MW00681890

THE WALL

Tours along the Former Border

Andreas Hoffmann and Matthias Hoffmann

THE WALL

Tours along the Former Border

nicolai

© 2003 Nicolaische Verlagsbuchhandlung GmbH, Berlin
All rights reserved
Original German edition:
Die Mauer. Touren entlang der ehemaligen Grenze
© 2003 Nicolaische Verlagsbuchhandlung GmbH, Berlin
Translation: Christine Shuttleworth, London
Cover: Pierre Adenis, G.A.F.F.
Photos: Matthias Hoffmann, Berlin (except pp. 6/7 and 125:
Erik-Jan Ouwerkerk, Berlin)
Maps: Bernd Matthes, Berlin
Sketch-map p. 13: Petra Müller
Lithography: LVD GmbH, Berlin
Printing and binding: Clausen & Bosse, Leck
ISBN 3-87584-988-4

CONTENTS

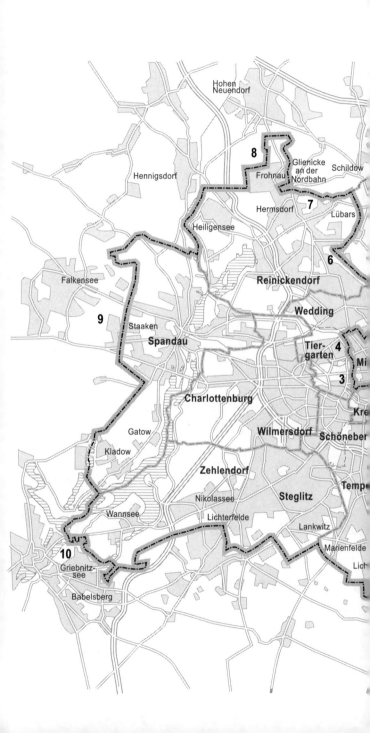

INTRODUCTION

HISTORY OF THE
BUILDING OF THE WALL

The Berlin Wall was a product of the Cold War that immediately followed the Second World War. In the Potsdam Agreement of August 1945, the four victorious powers, the USA, Britain, France and the Soviet Union, had divided Germany as well as Austria into zones. Berlin, like Vienna, had been split into four sectors, for which the respective military authorities were responsible. The two states and their capitals were to be treated as political and economic units. In Austria the State Treaty of 1955 put an end to the division of the country.

Not so in Germany. In Berlin an Allied Control Commission and an Allied Headquarters were established to coordinate the occupying powers with reference to Germany and specifically to Berlin. However, this failed because of the fundamentally conflicting ideologies and political approaches of the Western powers on the one hand and the Soviet Union on the other. Allied cooperation in Germany in practice ended with the currency reform, which resulted in the blockade of the Western sectors of Berlin, the political and administrative division of greater Berlin and the foundation of the Federal Republic of Germany as well as the German Democratic Republic in 1949.

The two German states, each soon integrated into the hostile blocs of world politics, developed separately: on the one hand political liberalism and social market economy, which resulted, with American credits, in an "economic miracle", on the other hand the loss of civil rights and a central planned economy, which, with the continuous economic exploitation by the Soviet Union, never functioned satisfactorily. As a result of the welfare differential, growing ever steeper, between the two German states, their differing concepts of freedom, and the well-nigh insatiable demand for labour forces of the Federal Republic's apparently endlessly booming market economy, between 1949 and 1961 more than 2.5 million inhabitants of the German Democratic Republic sought new homes in the West. In the first half of August 1961 alone, 159,730 individuals from the GDR, who had to leave behind their families, friends and colleagues, registered at the emergency reception camps specially set up for refugees. For each one, the decision to leave their homes, was momentous, dramatic, often bound up with personal sacrifice. For a national economy such as that of the GDR, the mass migration of its active workforce was a catastrophe.

THE GEOPOLITICAL SITUATION OF BERLIN

The sore point was Berlin. On the 1,381-kilometre-long border between the Federal Republic and the GDR, unrestricted traffic had already practically come to a standstill by 1952 because of formal obstacles such as entrance and exit permits, and roadblocks and patrol areas increasingly furnished with barbed wire fencing. The urban toing and froing in a lively metropolis of millions such as the four-sector city of Berlin on the other hand was more difficult to regulate. Daily, West Berliners travelled into the Eastern sector to make purchases, go to the hairdresser's or the theatre, while East Berliners, almost unsupervised, commuted across the border using the underground or S-Bahn (city and suburban trains) to their workplaces in the Western sectors, and in the evenings to the Western cinemas and shop windows – and thousands of migrants travelled in the same direction. Friedrich Ebert, the mayor of East Berlin, urged his West Berlin counterpart Willy Brandt to set up a commission to solve the refugee problem. Brandt refused. The GDR authorities were on their own in dealing with those who wanted to leave their state. Propaganda, dis-

INTRODUCTION

crimination against commuters over the border, and show trials of smugglers of GDR citizens out of the country and their recruiters and agents were ineffectual. More drastic measures had to be employed, involving structural changes. In the early morning of Sunday, 13 August 1961, some 10,000 members of the People's Army, 15,000 police officers and 12,000 members of workers' militia groups ensured that along the 43 kilometres or so of sector borders of Berlin (West) and the 112-kilometre-long border of the Potsdam district of the GDR, barbed wire was rolled out, traffic disrupted by the tearing up of the road surface, the through trains of the S-Bahn halted, and access to thirteen East Berlin underground stations forbidden.

THE BUILDING OF THE BORDER FORTIFICATIONS

As early as August 1961, construction began on a massive wall of concrete blocks. The windows and entrances to houses which – above all in the Bernauer Strasse between the districts of Wedding and Mitte – stood on the border area, were bricked up in October 1961, while the shafts of the sewerage system were barred and bridges were demolished.

After this, the appearance of the Berlin Wall was altered a number of times: in 1963 supervised building workers began to set up long, flat concrete sheets. From the early 1970s ready-made concrete parts, 3.7 metres high, were erected with pipes mounted on them, which were later "improved" by means of a version half a metre taller. In 1989 the wall extended around the Western sectors for a distance of 155 kilometres.

The form of the barrier varied according to the nature of the area to be cordoned off. Usually it consisted (from east to west) of a 2-metre-high wire-netting fence ("hinterland fence"), a signal fence of the same height, which if touched would give visual or acoustic warning of the escaper, surface or humped barriers to prevent vehicles getting through, observation and command towers (302 in number), bunkers (20) and areas for dogs to run (259), a lamp route with 5-metre-high lamp-posts, a columned route 3–4 metres wide navigable by means of open-topped Trabant military vehicles (typ Trabant 601 Kübel), a 6–15-metre-wide sandy control area, a ditch intended to prevent escape attempts by car, a concrete sheet wall up to 4.2 metres high, which seemed to lose its serious nature because of the graffiti on the other, West Berlin side, a strip about 6–8 metres wide which was actually part of the territory of East Berlin but was not accessible from there, and finally a mainly asphalted patrol path, which was used for patrolling along the border by the Western Allies as well as the West Berlin police. Each of the concrete sections, some 45,000 in all, weighed more than 2.5 tonnes, was 3.6 metres high and 1.2 metres wide. Land mines and automatic firing device facilities did not exist in Berlin. Seven checkpoints remained open, including Checkpoint Charlie, the so-called foreigners' crossing point.

Topography of the border fortifications

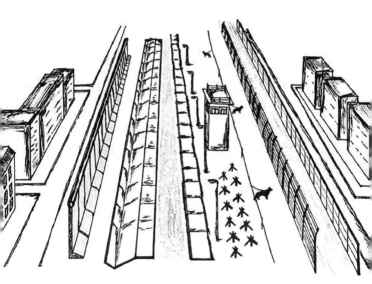

BORDER TRAFFIC

West Berliners were permitted visits to the other half of
the city without formality up to 23 August 1961. After
that, the intention of the GDR authorities was that these
should henceforth be allowed only with passes which
would be issued by employees of the GDR authorities in
West Berlin offices. The Senate felt that this violated the
status of Berlin as an area governed by the four powers,
and refused. This ended traffic across the border for all
Berliners.

It was not until the end of 1963 that a temporary regulation was instituted. With the passes that West Berliners had to obtain by standing for hours in the cold outside
the issuing offices, they were able to visit their friends
and relatives in East Berlin for one day. This procedure
was repeated in November 1964, at the turn of the year
from 1964 to 1965, at Easter and Whitsun of 1965, at
the turn of the year from 1965 to 1966, and finally at
Whitsun 1966. In "urgent family situations" (births, mar-
riages and deaths) further family visits were grudgingly
allowed. Pensioners in the GDR, however, were allowed
to leave from November 1964 onwards.

Apart from these exceptions, the reciprocal flow of
visitors dried up. Germans on different sides of the border were becoming strangers to each other. Only in the
phase of world-wide political détente did the federal
government succeed in softening the rigours of the division of Germany, bringing Germans on both sides of the
border closer to each other again by their "politics of small
steps".

With the signing of the Four Power Agreement in 1971
the Berlin Senate and the government of the GDR
agreed on an "alleviation and improvement of travel and
visitor traffic", which from June 1972 not only permitted
all residents of West Berlin to enter East Berlin, but for
the first time in twenty years also allowed GDR citizens
a stay of 30 days (from 1984, 45 days) a year, and even
overnight stays, as long as an invitation from Berlin or the
GDR was supplied in good time. The procedure for issu-

ing visas, at first very cumbersome, was simplified in the course of time; but the amount of money that had to be exchanged in the GDR at the non-market price of 1 : 1 was increased several times, on the last occasion to 25 Deutschmarks. The visa fees were paid by the federal government.

THE BUILDING OF THE WALL AND ITS CONSEQUENCES

The building of the Berlin Wall aroused dismay in Germany, above all where people were directly affected, were suddenly separated from their friends and relatives, or found their lifestyle destroyed. People in the GDR had the choice of leaving the country taken away from them. Somehow they had to come to terms with this. West Berlin had lost its surrounding area and gained a dubious tourist attraction. West Berliners were forced to realize with horror that their feelings about the building of the Wall were not shared in international political circles. The GDR government, which initiated the building work, repeatedly stressed that the "anti-fascist protective barrier" (to use their terminology) had made peace in the Europe of the Cold War safer. The two world powers saw this in a similar way. The Soviet government had given its approval to the building of the Wall, although the representatives of the Warsaw Pact had pronounced against it because of their fear of loss of prestige, which in fact proved the case. The fortified border ended the American "roll-back" policy, the driving back of Communism, at least in central Europe. The US government saw in the building of the Wall the end of the Berlin crisis, which had been smouldering since the Soviet government's ultimatum in 1958 in the form of a demand for a demilitarized, neutral, autonomous political entity in West Berlin. Kennedy, contrary to all public statements, had less objection to the Wall insofar as his Soviet opponents appeared to recognize the rights of the Western Allies in the Western sectors and also respected the access routes to Berlin. The protests of the Western Allies

INTRODUCTION

against the violation of the four-power status of Berlin accordingly arrived somewhat late – a full four days after the event. Chancellor Konrad Adenauer, preoccupied with the Bundestag election, managed only after nine days to fly to Berlin. For his policy for Germany, the building of the Wall was a disaster. At the Bundestag election, a full month later, his party lost its absolute majority.

Looking back, historians regard 13 August 1961 as the second birth of the GDR. In the shadow of the Wall, it was able to consolidate itself. While the fluctuation of the population had at first been brought forcibly to a halt, it now seemed possible in the workers' and farmers' state to put their ideal into practice: the Socialist community of people. Indeed, "Socialism existing in real terms" enabled GDR citizens to enjoy an unusually high material and social standard of living. However, at no time could the GDR stand comparison with its more liberal and prosperous capitalist neighbour state.

Dissidents could no longer leave the socialist state, as they still could in 1961. No fundamental criticism could be expressed either; basic rights, which would have been needed in order to do so, were not recognized here. The government was unable to make good use of the salutary lessons of open criticism. On the contrary: criticism, however benevolently intended, was suppressed.

THE END OF THE WALL

A political unit cannot be either constructed or maintained by rhetoric means. Encouraged by the liberalisation of state and society taking place in the Soviet Union during the mid-80s, critical voices, in the GDR too, had become ever louder, and loudest of all since the beginning of September 1989 at the Monday demonstrations in Leipzig. The demand for freedom to travel was particularly vehement. The Wall was the obstacle to this. As an archaic instrument of separation, it was no longer appropriate in view of the changed political situation within the Eastern bloc. The Iron Curtain first began to corrode on 27 June 1989 when the barbed wire was officially cut

An "open door" in the Wall (Ebertstrasse, 1987)

at Sopron on the border between Hungary and Austria. Thousands of GDR citizens travelled to Hungary; others occupied the Federal German Embassies in Prague and Warsaw in order to achieve their goal of travel to the Federal Republic.

When, at 18.57 on 9 November 1989 Günter Schabowski, a member of the "Politbüro" of the SED (Socialist Unity Party of Germany), announced in a somewhat casual manner at a press conference, "Private journeys out of the country can be applied for without preconditions such as travel passes or family relationships. Permission will be granted at short notice", there was no holding the Berliners. Tailbacks formed at the checkpoints. At 23.14, at the Bornholmer Strasse checkpoint, an employee of the border troops opened the first barrier, and during that night and the days that followed, Germans celebrated their reunification, almost eleven months before it was officially in force. The wall crum-

---

bled under the hammer-blows of souvenir-hunters, known as "Mauerspechte", the street and train connections were gradually restored, and with the coming into effect of the inter-state agreement between the two Germanys on 1 July 1990, the personal checks at the borders, which had practically been abandoned already, were officially halted. On 3 October 1990 the German Democratic Republic joined the Federal Republic of Germany; the reunification was also legally confirmed.

DEALING WITH THE HERITAGE OF THE WALL

Every segment of the Wall, which was initially removed by cranes, every checkpoint that was opened as a result, every link road that once again became accessible to traffic, every rail connection that was restored, was cheered by the population during those first weeks and months. Every piece of concrete, every section of wire fencing less meant more liberation. In early 1990 the GDR government and the East Berlin city council decided on the total demolition of the border complexes. This was ceremonially initiated on 13 June 1990 and concluded with equal ceremony on 30 November 1990. The much more extensive demolition work on the Berlin-Brandenburg border was not completed for several more months. Parts of the Wall were placed under a preservation order as early as 1990, other parts not until 2001. Even today the Wall's status as a historic monument is questioned when remains of the Wall stand in the way of a profitable site development.

The dispute about the restitution of the Wall sites too has still not been resolved. The properties in question on the Wall area were compulsorily expropriated, and the residents rehoused. The question of restitution and compensation for those affected was not covered by the "Agreement between the Federal Republic of Germany and the German Democratic Republic on the creation of German unity – Unification agreement" signed on 31 August 1990. The "Law on the Sale of Wall and Border Sites to the Former Owners (Wall Site Law)* of 15 July 1996 rules that an expropriated owner will only be entitled to the return of the property by paying 25 per cent of the current value, and if the Federal government does not want to use it for urgent public purposes or sell it to a third party in the public interest. In such a case compensation of 75 per cent of the value of the site is payable.

For the tourist industry, the removal of the Wall represented a problem. The city had lost an attraction which was unique in the world. Today, there is no area, even in places where parts of the Wall have been preserved, where the brutality of the division can be comprehended. For the most part, the course of the border can no longer be seen in the reunited city – unless of course one knows where to look. The following ten tours of the Wall invite you to develop a sharper eye and to keep the memory of the Wall alive.

TOUR 1

FROM HEIDELBERGER STRASSE
TO THE SCHLESISCHER BUSCH

Treptower Strasse – Heidelberger Strasse – Bouchéstrasse – Harzer Strasse –
Canal-side road by the Landwehrkanal – Flutgraben – Vor dem Schlesischen
Tor – Schlesische Strasse – Schlesisches Tor underground station

Distance: 6 kilometres
Time: 2 hours

The parts of the city that we will pass through on the following tour of the Wall are among the most densely
populated areas of Europe. The forcible separation of
Neukölln (formerly West Berlin) and Treptow (formerly
East Berlin) would seem incredible if history had not
proved it possible – at least, for 29 years, as long as the
Wall still stood.

The starting point of our tour is the Treptower Strasse/
Harzer Strasse stop on the 141 bus route. We will follow
Treptower Strasse northwards. It ends as a cul-de-sac at
Heidelberger Strasse – a clear indication that the Wall
once formed a barrier there. In its shadow, in the midst
of a "protected green space", a children's playground and
day centre have been created.

We turn left at Heidelberger Strasse. It is easy to find
the area where the Wall stood. It is marked by a double
row of paving stones on the road surface. The borderline
is delineated as before in the urban landscape: an area
of wasteland extends along Treptower and Heidelberger
Strasse – formerly on the Treptow side, that is, the former "eastern" side.

Few parts of Berlin demonstrate so clearly in what a
narrow space the Wall cut the city and the residential
areas in two. The actual concrete wall ran alongside the
kerb on the left-hand side of Heidelberger Strasse. The
pavement in front of it, according to the land register, also
belonged to East Berlin, but was actually on the West
Berlin side of the Wall. The residents of Neukölln illegally

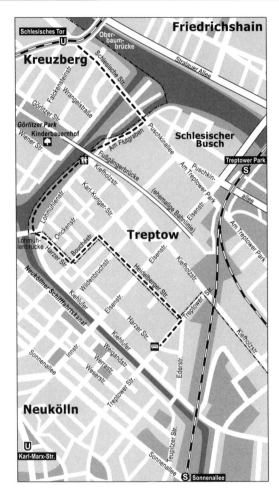

parked their cars there, reaching the entrances to their houses through the recultivated front gardens. But where the pavement bordered directly on the building line, the tenants were able to reach their homes only through the houses on the side street and from there via the courtyards at the back. Things were even more complicated on the East Berlin side. The actual border strip occupied the entire width of the street. The houses on its right were already in the security zone that extended as far as the Kiefholzstrasse, running northwards in parallel.

The residential house at 79–81 Heidelberger Strasse, which we are about to pass, for example, was on the list for demolition in the mid-80s. Today, painted dark green, the house towers up in the former border area, which is still clearly to be discerned.

In 1980 the city council of East Berlin investigated 170 houses with 2,551 apartments in the border zone. In Treptow alone there were 27 houses with 493 apartments. Access was permitted only with the appropriate passes. No problem for the residents – but what about guests? Special passes had to be procured for them in the event of a party. But what if one ran out of coal for heating, or if a water-pipe burst? Selected physicians and businesses known to the residents were provided with so-called permanent passes for the "strengthening of law and order in the border area".

Who would want to reside and live under these conditions? In 1982 the city council recognized the problem: "The fluctuation of the border population must be more decisively countered in co-operation with the commanding officers and leaders of the armed defensive forces with a view to developing firm and politically stable households. The registration of apartments standing empty in the border zone, their repair and speedy reallocation according to the legal requirements are to be permanently ensured. The standard house rules for the border area must be explained to the residents and their enforcement must be closely monitored."

The city council was also concerned about the image of the area near the border. Many houses had been so severely neglected that in 1980 the city fathers of East Berlin urged: "This situation affects not only the citizens who have lived there for years, personally, but also the reactions of the class enemies in respect of the denigration of Socialism actually existing in the GDR, because of the condition of the buildings in the border zone."

The red-brick building on the northern side of the street, also in the former border zone, was part of the "Werk für Sicherungs- und Signaltechnik Berlin" (Works for Protection and Signal Engineering, Berlin), who were outfitters to the GDR railway system. With an extension added after reunification, Siemens-Transportation System Berlin today preserves the business tradition of this site.

On the corner of Elsenstrasse a memorial was unveiled on 13 August 2001 in honour of Heinz Jercha, who gave aid to refugees. At 27 years of age, he conducted 25 East Berliners through a 30-metre-long escape tunnel through to the West. In doing so, he lost his own life on 27 March 1962, shot by border guards.

On the corner of Bouchéstrasse, which we now enter from the left, the former border area still lies waste, as with other locations. Here (seen from west to east) crowded together in a narrow space the Wall, a scrapyard for motor vehicles together with anti-tank obstacles, the traffic route, the rows of streetlamps and, on the undeveloped sites between the Treptow houses, the hinterland wall.

Number 33 Bouchéstrasse, corner of Schmollerstrasse, on 31 March 1983: two electricians, both in their mid-twenties, are working in the house, they spend the night there and wake up as it is getting light. They fasten the end of a nylon rope to the roof, and with a bow and arrow shoot the other end over the wall, where a helper catches hold of it, pulls it taut and fastens it. Pulleys are attached, and soon the two young men are speeding 40 metres from the roof down towards Neukölln.

Let us pause briefly at number 37 Bouchéstrasse. An obscure arrow on the house number-plate indicates that the entrance to this dwelling-house is on the other side – unavoidably, since the original entrance is clearly seen to be bricked up. The street lamp, higher than the others, formerly lit up the border area, as also, incidentally, did the one at 31 Bouchéstrasse. It was on the asphalted pavement, which still, significantly, turns off right at Harzer Strasse, that the border troops were on patrol.

TOUR 1

The residents of the house had no business there.

We now follow the former route of the Wall to the right into Harzer Strasse. After about 200 metres we reach Lohmühlenplatz, and now things get tricky in typical Berlin style: we are standing at the "Lohmühlen-Zwickel". Here the concrete Wall ran in a direct line from Harzer Strasse to the canal. Nevertheless a small "Zwickel" (wedge-shaped area) in front of the Wall belonged to East Berlin. This caused some difficulty, for no one was allowed to use the Lohmühlenbrücke, neither vehicles nor pedestrians. The latter were at least granted a makeshift footbridge, still in existence, a few metres east of the Lohmühlenbrücke. But motorists, in order to get from the Kiehlufer to the opposite bank of the Neukölln ship canal, had to put up with a troublesome detour. In the course of an exchange of areas, the "Zwickel" was snipped off and on 1 July 1988 became part of Neukölln, and the traffic route over the bridge was quickly re-established.

We will not use the bridge, but saunter among cherry-trees on the green bank of the Landwehrkanal on the near side. Here people take their dogs for walks, kids are let loose to romp round, volleyball players smash into the net, and nearby, pale breasts are exposed to the sun. Peaceful activity as far as the eye can see. Who still remembers the border area right by the canal bank? "Under the branches of the cherry trees in blossom, no one is a stranger here", reads an inscription on the Lohmühlenbrücke. The trees were a Japanese gift to the city. Normality has returned to this once frighteningly quiet corner of the Wall. And so has noise. "Hardly anyone ever used to lose their way and end up here," says a local woman. That was when it was still quiet, in the heart of the city.

When the green space by the canal bank was laid out, from 1997 to 2000, the rolling-home-owners had to give way. We find the city nomads in a circle of wagons near the old railway bridge, where we can enjoy refreshing cold drinks. In summer, the young people even organise an open-air cinema.

Across the Berlin-Görlitz railway bridge, on the Kreuzberg side of the Landwehrkanal, lies Görlitzer Park. Here an echo of Berlin railway history can be heard. In 1867 the first passenger trains ran from here to Görlitz, on 29 April 1951 the last one. In 1967 the reception hall was blown up, though the goods station continued in use. An iron gate blocked off the bridge. For every "interzone goods train" the employees of the Eastern transport police had to open the gate, which was closed again after the last carriage had passed. On 31 March 1962 one of the transport police officers closed it behind him, and there he was in the West. After July 1985 there was no longer any goods traffic here, and the Kreuzberg district authority had the railway tracks grassed over. In this district which had not exactly been blessed by nature, a park had been gained. Since the fall of the Wall, the inhabitants of Treptow have been able to use it too.

Lohmühlen-
brücke (still
closed in 1986)

TOUR 1

Further along the Landwehrkanal, we reach the next bridge. In the course of Lohmühlenstrasse, the Treptower Brücke had since 1852 crossed the Flutgraben. Belonging to West Berlin, after 1961 it ended directly at the Wall. On the Kreuzberg side this rendered Lohmühlenstrasse useless. In 1978 it was turned into a children's playground.

Leaving the bridge on our left, we cross wide expanses of lawn to the "Schlesischer Busch", a little wood, the remains of a larger forest, which building speculators had had cleared in the 1830s. In the middle of this grove, in Puschkinallee, is an old watch tower of the "Führungsstelle" type.

The tower at the "Schlesischer Busch" is under a preservation order – and it is empty. It is in urgent need of renovation, but the Köpenick-Treptow district, which owns it, does not have the estimated sum necessary, 40 000 euros. The association for the Museum of Forbidden Art, which organised some 40 exhibitions here over a ten-year period, was closed down in 2000.

On the opposite side of Puschkinallee, since 11 November 1989 once again the main transport connection between Kreuzberg and Treptow, border troops were once quartered on the present company premises of the Berlin branch of the NISSAN car firm. Here an area of

"FÜHRUNGS-STELLEN"

Four towers that functioned as "Führungsstellen" still exist in the Berlin area: in Hennigsdorf, near Hohen Neuendorf (see Tour 8: From Frohnau to Frohnau), at Kieler Eck (see Tour 4: From Sandkrugbrücke to Nordbahnhof) and at the "Schlesischer Busch". Several other watchtowers were linked to these towers, about 9 metres high, and the electrical border security complexes were observed. On the ground floor were the sanitary installations as well as a small kitchen, on the first floor a room for accommodation with two double bunk beds for up to four border soldiers. On the second floor was the actual guardroom, which was usually manned by two guards. They monitored the border in their district on electric boards as well as any signals set off on the contact fences.

whitewashed hinterland wall forms the border of the site. The original border lamp-posts still exist.

To the west, we cross the Flutgraben via the Obere Freiarchenbrücke. Strange places: one of the oldest German petrol stations, built in 1928, under a preservation order. On the street called Vor dem Schlesischen Tor, exactly three house-numbers in length, is Berlin's last tax office, a brick building placed at the city limits in 1861. Next to it is the top sluice-gate of the Landwehrkanal where it flows into the Spree. And in the Flutgraben, until reunification, carp, trout and pike, our favourite freshwater fish, were kept in old wooden barges for the firm of Walter Hoffmeister. Since then, the local pub "Freischwimmer" has been established here. The beer tastes particularly good on warm summer evenings.

Via Schlesische Strasse, 700 metres further on, we reach the U-Bahn station Schlesisches Tor. At number 44, Falckensteinstrasse, we read the inscription "Café im Grenzbereich" (café in the border area). Today it stands empty. Here, only yesterday it seems, two worlds collided.

TOUR 2

FROM OBERBAUMBRÜCKE
TO SPITTELMARKT

Schlesisches Tor U-Bahn station – Bevernstrasse – Gröbenufer –
Oberbaumbrücke – Mühlenstrasse – Stralauer Platz – Schillingbrücke –
Engel-/Bethaniendamm – Leuschnerdamm – Waldemarstrasse –
Luckauer Strasse – Sebastianstrasse – Alexandrinenstrasse –
Stallschreiberstrasse – Alte Jakobstrasse (through Seydelstrasse to
Spittelmarkt U-Bahn station)

Distance: 6.5 kilometres
Time: 3 hours

"WARNING – MORTAL DANGER! Waterway is the property of the Eastern sector of Berlin!" A board at the
corner of Gröbenufer and Bevernstrasse, the departure
point for our tour, warned in German and Turkish:
"DIKKAT ÖLÜM TEHLIKESI". There was a serious background to the warning.

11 May 1975. The Kreuzberg fire station is summoned
to the Gröbenufer. A boy has fallen into the Spree while
playing. Four minutes later, help is at hand. But they are
not allowed to rescue the child. The Spree is foreign territory, and sovereignty rights apply. The GDR border
guards call their own divers, who of course arrive too late.
Five-year-old Çetin is dead.

This was the fifth fatal case of this kind. There was
general bitterness. And so only five months later the
Berlin senate and the GDR government came to an
"Agreement on rescue measures in certain accidents at
sections of the border waters". But Çetin could have
been saved, for this problem had already come under
discussion as early as 1973, but the discussions broke
down because of the question of political status. Was the
Spree an "inland water" within the four sectors (as the
Senate maintained), or a "border water" between the GDR
and West Berlin (as the GDR government claimed)?

The posts to which this board was fixed are still there, by the way. Today, they bear the timetable of the pleasure boats which have been allowed to moor here again since 1990. On the steps of the old mooring, a stone block is dedicated to "The unknown refugee". One of them is known: Hans Räwel, shot on the morning of New Year's Day 1963 from a patrol boat. Another, still nameless, drowned on 19 January 1965.

In the 18th century the Oberbaumbrücke, which lies in front of us, marked the city limits (information board on the corner of Gröbenufer). At night, floating tree trunks closed off the Oberspree. The bridge of today, modelled on a city gate in the Mark of Brandenburg from the days of brick Gothic, has only been there since 1896; the overhead railway has been running since 1902. Destroyed in the Second World War, the bridge was speedily repaired, though not its towers and arches. On 13 August 1961 all traffic across the bridge came to an end, and the carriageway and arches were bricked up. But before Christmas 1963 the border guard opened a "little door" underneath: Berlin's eighth border crossing-point, for pedestrians only. The little checkpoint buildings stood at the northern (that is, the "eastern") bridgehead. In 1972 the checkpoint was removed. Since November 1994, cars have once again been able to cross the

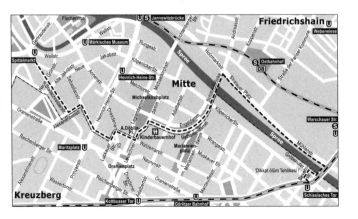

bridge, and some day trams will also be able to do so. As yet, the tramlines on the bridge go nowhere. The overhead railway, however, has been running above the restored arches since 14 October 1995. Since 1997, "Stein – Papier – Schere" ("Stone – paper – scissors"), a neon installation by the artist Thorsten Goldberg at the central thoroughfare across the Oberbaumbrücke, has given visual expression to the former border crossing point.

On 12 August 1961 there were sector crossings on 81 streets, a day later there were only twelve, and from 23 August a mere seven. The GDR's minister of the interior specified precisely who might use them, in order to make it absolutely clear that West Berlin was not part of the Federal Republic:

BORDER CROSSING POINTS

- Checkpoint Charlie (Friedrichstrasse) for the Allies, foreigners and the Diplomatic Corps;
- Bornholmer and Heinrich-Heine-Strasse for goods traffic from west to east, and citizens of the Federal Republic (from 1972 the Bornholmer Strasse was also open to West Berliners);
- Chaussee-, Invalidenstrasse and Sonnenallee only for West Berliners;
- Friedrichstrasse station for everyone travelling by city and suburban railway or (from 1964) by underground.
- From Christmas 1963 the eighth border crossing was opened at the Oberbaumbrücke (for pedestrians only).

At the border to the district of Potsdam, vehicles in transit formed a tailback on the motorway at Dreilinden/Drewitz and on Heerstrasse. In 1972 these two crossings, as well as the new one at Waltersdorfer Chaussee, were also open for travel into the GDR. In 1987, a new border crossing opened at Heiligensee/Stolpe on the new motorway to Hamburg. The border stations for long-distance traffic were Griebnitzsee and (from 1976) Staaken. Transit shipping and (from 1978) transport of building rubble by water was supervised in Babelsberg; in addition, West Berlin refuse trucks passed the border at Kirchhainer Damm.

The East Side Gallery begins at the renovated Spree Warehouse, in Mühlenstrasse. At 1,200 metres it is the longest open-air gallery in the world. The concrete walls still standing here formed the hinterland wall, which closed off the border area from the eastern part of the city. After the Wall had lost its power to terrify, artists from various countries worked on it in such a convincing manner that in 1991 this part of it was placed under a preservation order, and in 2000 it was restored. On Strasse der Pariser Kommune, we pass through an old access gate to the former border area on the banks of the Spree behind the Gallery. Here we discover, on the neighbouring commercial site, the oldest border wall in Berlin with pieces of broken glass embedded in it.

Leaving Ostbahnhof, one of Berlin's mainline stations, on the right, we pass Stralauer Platz, formerly a restful park complex. A former landmark in its centre, the Andreaskirche, a church built in 1856, was destroyed in the Second World War and the area was levelled off in 1949 (the parish hall, 32 Stralauer Platz). The neighbouring building in clinker brick with the coat of arms of the city of Berlin and the date 1908 on the façade (number 33/34), on the other hand, was renovated. It served as a central storehouse for the city gasworks, whose second oldest production complex was close by on the Spree embankment, on the Schillingbrücke.

In 2001 a hotel and luxury flats were built on one side next to the renovated brick gasworks buildings. On the other side, on the corner of Stralauer Platz, remains of the Berlin Wall have been preserved. On 14 February 1972, just before midnight, 29-year-old Manfred Weylandt was shot dead here by border troops as he was trying to swim across the Spree.

The name of the Schillingbrücke, privately financed in 1840, has a double meaning. The main investor was a master bricklayer working for the court, Johann Friedrich Schilling, who gave the bridge its name, and those who passed over it paid half a schilling. In 1871/72, the wooden bridge, now the property of the city, was restored in stone, and in 1911 it was widened. From 1945 it

belonged to the Soviet sector, and after 13 August 1961 it was closed to traffic – except for the open-topped Trabant 601s, the border brigades' patrol vehicles.

Patches of tar in the road surface of Bethanien-damm (2002)

The Spree formed the border only as far as the Schillingbrücke. Here it turned off to the south-west, blocked off Köpenicker Strasse (left from the traffic lights) and continued in a broad curve to Bethanien-damm, which, along with its pavement, belonged to East Berlin. Patches of tar at regular intervals in the cobble-stones of Engeldamm as well as in the road surface of Bethaniendamm show where the concrete posts of the barbed-wire fence were embedded in August 1961. The "modern Wall" (made of the well-known concrete slabs) replaced it in the 1970s. The edge between the old and new street surface shows exactly where it stood. The pavement in front of it and a strip of six to eight metres of East Berlin territory could only be used by West Berliners, even though this was unauthorised.

Bethaniendamm borders on the site of the former deaconesses' residence Bethanien (built in 1845–47 by Ludwig Persius, Friedrich August Stüler and Theodor

Stein) with its hospital, in operation until 1970. The empty building was occupied in 1971 by young people and students in an operation that attracted public attention and saved it from the threat of demolition. Today Bethanien houses artistic and social institutions.

Nearby, on Christmas Day 1963, two young men tried to climb over the Wall. One was successful, but his friend, Paul Schultz, was shot dead. Two other GDR citizens succeeded in escaping on 28 September 1988 while under fire; one woman was arrested.

The green space between the parallel streets Bethaniendamm and Engeldamm (Fritz-Heckert-Strasse from 1951 to 1991) formed the border area. Both streets formed part of the embankment of the Luisenstädtischer Kanal, which had been laid out in 1848–52 to the plans of the landscape gardener Peter Joseph Lenné. In the late 1920s the canal was drained and remodelled, after 1945 the new park was largely levelled off with rubble. The old clinker embankment walls emerge in Adalbertstrasse. In the 1980s the old park was restored in Kreuzberg between the canal walls, and in 1993 the same work began in the Mitte district.

Visually effective, churches formed so-called *points de vue* by the canal: the Protestant Thomaskirche (1864–69; architect, Friedrich Adler) on the left with its two towers, completely restored in the 1990s, and a few hundred metres further to the right, the Catholic St Michael Kirche (1851–56; architect, August Soller), since 1944 an impressive ruin in the North Italian Renaissance style.

On the other, "eastern" side, numbers 62–64 Engeldamm, we are struck by a neo-Gothic brick building from 1902 which has been transformed into an office and residential building. It was from here that the "Berliner Gewerkschaftskommission" (trade union organisation) organised the workers' struggles during the last days of the empire. When the Berlin Wall stood in front of its entrance, the former trade union offices housed the patients of the City Hospital of the Mitte district. In 1927 the transport workers' union commissioned Bruno Taut to design the union house at 70 Engeldamm (today the seat of the union ver.di), which his brother Max completed by 1930. It was here that, up to the 1980s, the FDGB, the executive of the GDR federation of trade unions, had its seat.

The street turns left into Leuschnerdamm. Here, on 29 April 1963, four men managed to drive a four-metre-wide gap in the Wall with a military lorry, and then make their escape through it. Equally successful was the flight of a couple from number 13 Leuschnerdamm, in the late summer of 1961. The husband, who had been employed to work on the Berlin Wall, was brought his lunch by his wife. In a flash, he pulled her up onto the Wall, and both leaped into the "West". When the border guards began to shoot at them, a dust-cart driver put his vehicle into reverse, driving into the firing line. The couple were saved.

There are many relics of the border to be found here: the patches of tar in the road surface, with the sawn-off iron posts from the first generation of the Wall, and in the front gardens the wooden lamp-posts, still in use today. But the tenants of the houses on Leuschnerdamm no longer have to use Waldemarstrasse and its courtyards in order to get to their apartments; once again they are able to use the pavement that used to belong to East Berlin. And the Engelbecken (angel basin) of the Luisenstädtischer Kanal, that they see from their windows, once again contains water, in which the heavens are reflected.

The Wall turned to the north at the bridge. After the canal over which it had led up during the 1920s had been filled in, the bridge was hardly recognisable. At Oranienplatz too, some 300 metres away, there was a bridge over the canal. But nothing, it seems, can bridge the gap over which police and demonstrators clash, year in, year out, regularly on 1 May.

The view from the border area to the right of Waldemar Strasse has been open since the end of January 1990, that is since a major section of the Wall between Leuschnerdamm and Luckauer Strasse was demol-

Warning at Leuschnerdamm: Keep off the pavement! (1986)

ished. Since then, this area has awaited a convincing urban development plan.

From Alfred-Döblin-Platz onwards, the course of the Wall can be recognised from a double row of paving-stones in the road surface. Opposite the sites at numbers 79–82 Sebastianstrasse, four border lighting systems have been transformed into normal street lamps. Behind them are the rows and rows of houses of the Heinrich Heine estate, which, begun in 1958, was in the process of being built when the Wall was erected.

The Heinrich-Heine-Strasse was known as a border checkpoint – only for "citizens of the Federal Republic of Germany", not for "citizens from West Berlin". According to the GDR government, these were citizens of two different states. Commercial traffic was also allowed to pass through the checkpoint (see the information board on the corner of Prinzen- and Sebastianstrasse). Today, a trader offers second-hand cars for sale on the site of the checkpoint buildings. Who today still remembers the attempts to escape?

18 April 1962. Klaus Brüske is driving a lorry with two colleagues on board, along Heinrich-Heine-Strasse towards the border. Suddenly he speeds up. At the zigzag roadblocks, the guards open fire. Brüske is hit, and collapses. The dying man holds his course towards Kreuzberg. The vehicle arrives at its destination. The passengers are wounded, Brüske dies. Another escape attempt by car fails on Boxing Day 1965. The driver, Heinz Schönberger, is killed, the other three people in the car are arrested.

In Sebastianstrasse we can continue to follow the Wall markings. Numbers 69–73 were built set back from the road, so that, beside the pavement, which according to the land register belonged to East Berlin, it was possible to build a new pedestrian path as part of West Berlin, thus gaining a little green space.

The houses on Alexandrinenstrasse date from an earlier period. They belong to a residential estate which was built at the same time as the Heinrich Heine estate. In 1958 it was named after the late Governing Mayor of Berlin, Otto Suhr.

The old road surface that used to belong to the border area pokes out under the edges of the newly applied bitumen. For the street itself, a new road open to vehicles was created on the Kreuzberg side. In the middle of the overgrown border area on Alexandrinenstrasse, we have no difficulty in finding the old tarred traffic road. It leads us around the Luisenstadt Primary School. A glance upwards shows that there are still bars on the windows of the gym.

From Alexandrinenstrasse, the Wall ran to the right into Stallschreiberstrasse. Here too, a new access road was needed for the residents, for the old street, still present in a fragmentary form, disappeared into the border area. A clear view was created a few metres away in 1964 by blowing up the ruins of the Luisenstadtkirche (consecrated in 1695, known until 1802 as the Sebastianskirche). Even before this time the site had not been particularly inviting. It was here that plague victims and poor people had been laid to rest. Let us leave them in peace. Our tour ends at Alte Jakobstrasse.

FROM SPITTELMARKT
TO THE REICHSTAG

Axel-Springer-Strasse – Zimmerstrasse – Niederkirchnerstrasse –
Stresemannstrasse – Ebertstrasse – Friedrich-Ebert-Platz

Distance : 4 kilometres
Time: 4 hours (including visit to the Wall Museum at Checkpoint Charlie)

Our tour of the Wall begins on the corner of Beuth-
strasse and Axel-Springer-Strasse, as the former Lindenstrasse has been called in this area since 1996. Coming
from Spittelmarkt U-Bahn station, we pass a row of
high-rise buildings which were built in the mid-1970s on
the south side of Leipziger Strasse as a town-planning
defence against West Berlin.

A double row of paving-stones marks the course of
the Wall along Lindenstrasse. As early as 270 years ago
it had already formed a border, that of Friedrichstadt, a
shelter for refugees. Frederick III, Elector of Brandenburg, gave orders for the building of this city in 1688, and
in 1709 it was united with Berlin. Huguenots, who were
persecuted for their beliefs in France, found refuge here.
We follow the paving-stone markings to the right into
Zimmerstrasse, the southernmost street in Friedrichstadt before it was widened in 1734. The name of the
street (Carpenters' Street) comes from that period of
Baroque building mania, when the carpenters used to
store their materials here.

At the next crossroads the offices of the publishers
Springer-Verlag, founded in 1966, turns its windowless
gables towards the former border, intended as a kind of
protest by the free press. It stands in a historic row of
houses and once seperated Jerusalemer Strasse as did
the Wall and the residential estate on the Leipziger
Strasse. Next to it, on the site of the former Scherl-Ver-
lag (an important publishing house), a printing works

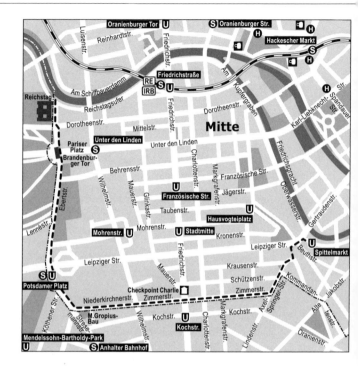

was created there in 1959, 150 metres long, flat in out-line, which was replaced in 2001/2002 by the present structure. In 1968 it was the target of fiery student protests against journalistic bias.

It was from the Springer site that, in the spring of 1962, four young men dug a tunnel to the cellar of num-ber 56 Jerusalemer Strasse, to help their relatives es-cape to the West. The attempt succeeded on 18 June 1962, but a GDR border soldier, Reinhold Huhn, lost his life. A commemorative plaque and a memorial were set up a few paces to the north, on the corner of Jerusalemer and Schützenstrasse (known between 1966 and 1991 as Reinhold-Huhn-Strasse), in his honour and that of the members of GDR border troops killed at the Wall. Huhn's case remained unsolved for a long time; Western news-papers wrote of "trigger-happy Vopos [GDR police officers]", while those in the GDR referred to "murderous agents of the West". It was not until 1999 that the Berlin regional court sentenced a pensioner to one year in prison for manslaughter. He had been one of the tunnel-diggers as a young man, and had confessed to shooting Reinhold Huhn.

On Zimmerstrasse, only a few houses had survived the Second World War unscathed. It was not possible to close the large gaps in the cityscape until after reunification. The town houses completed in 1997 on the north side of the street form an interesting example of one of the last works of Aldo Rossi, who died in the same year. This star architect from Milan conceived the ensemble (small plots of land divided into working and living quarters) as a homage to the architecture of late-19th-century Berlin. And in the back courtyard of number 67, Zimmerstrasse, anyone who would like to indulge in a few minutes of *Gemütlichkeit* can order a cup of coffee.

In 1999, a 2.4-metre-high rusty metal column created by the sculptor Karl Biedermann in front of number 26 Zimmerstrasse replaced an earlier wooden cross, erected in memory of the cruel death of Peter Fechter. This cross, which was sawn off in 1995 by a self-styled "New People's Army of the GDR" in "memory of the fallen, of the border troops persecuted by the imperialism of the Federal Republic, and the victims of the fall of the Wall", is preserved in the Wall Museum at Checkpoint Charlie. On 17 August 1962, towards 2.15 pm, Fechter, a young building worker, had tried to climb over the Wall with a friend. The friend succeeded, but Fechter was shot, fell back behind the Wall and lay bleeding to death for 50 minutes, pleading more and more weakly for help. (A notice on the corner of Charlottenstrasse tells the story.) During the days that followed, fights broke out between angry Berliners and both Soviet and US troops. These, as well as the West Berlin police, were accused of not having come to Fechter's aid. But it was the guards of the 1st Border Brigade who were mainly responsible. On 5 March 1997, the Berlin regional court passed a suspended sentence on two of them, by then 55 and 61 years old, of 20 and 21 months respectively, for joint mans-laughter. In the judge's opinion, it had been proved that Fechter died, not from the failure to give him medical help, but from the gunshot wound. It was no longer possible to find out who had held the deadly weapon.

The checkpoint on the corner of Friedrichstrasse became famous under its American name: Checkpoint Charlie (see the information on the walls). The name comes from the American alphabetic code: C for Charlie. "Alpha" referred to the Helmstedt border crossing, "Bravo" to Dreilinden. Checkpoint Charlie was created in 1961 exclusively for foreigners, diplomats and relatives of the Allies. Should they be monitored? If so, that would have been the end of the Four Powers' sovereignty over the whole of Berlin. On 15 October 1961, there was a confrontation. GDR guards refused entry to US citizens who would not provide identification. On 25 October it happened again. Then American tanks drove up and forced an entry for US citizens across the sector boundary. On 27 October Soviet tanks too took up their positions – a moment of significance in world history. It is the only direct military confrontation between the two superpowers by land that has ever taken place.

The little guards' hut on the central strip of Friedrichstrasse behind the sandbags filled with concrete is an attempt to create the atmosphere of those days. However, it lacks authenticity, for it is only a replica of the little hut that was put together there on 22 September 1961. In 1976 it was replaced by a larger structure, which was removed on 22 June 1990 by a crane, when the border operations were abandoned in the presence of the two German foreign ministers and those of the four Allied powers. The replica was unveiled on 13 August 2000. It is towered over by portraits of a Russian and an American soldier, a work commissioned from the artist Frank Thiel under the auspices of the Senate's programme "Kunst im Stadtraum" ("Art in Urban Space").

Since 1963, authentic material has been on display at the Wall Museum at Checkpoint Charlie (open daily from 9 am to 10 pm).

Replica of the first guards' hut at Checkpoint Charlie (2002)

On the other hand, the "original" caps and badges offered by street traders as souvenirs resemble the US uniforms in which on 19 December 1965, an extremely nervous couple from the GDR, engaged to be married, passed through the Allied checkpoint without being checked. The Ford was genuine, as was its stolen American registration number, but the uniforms were copies. However, escapes were not always successful. In 1973 and 1974, deserting comrades were shot by border troops. On 5 January 1974, one of them had taken an officer hostage, driving him along in front of himself with a drawn pistol.

In May 1986 the American pacifist John Runnings came from Seattle to Berlin to campaign at Checkpoint Charlie against the Wall and for peace. He had two plans for attracting public attention: first, to climb the Berlin Wall from West to East, and secondly to get himself taken into custody. He achieved his first aim on 9 June and 7 August 1986. Each time he climbed to the top of the Wall by means of a ladder, undertook a walk, and in the process broke the pipe on the Wall in pieces, using a sledgehammer. Border troops pulled him down and interrogated him. He was not imprisoned. A member of the US consulate staff in West Berlin came to collect him and brought him back. Runnings did not give up. Again and again he went back to Checkpoint Charlie, to paint the Wall, hand out leaflets, display posters and to provoke the border troops (but also the Western police and military police). On 25 October he was successful at last: he was sentenced to ten days in prison. On 18 November he climbed the Wall again and was again, as he wished, imprisoned, this time for two months. He was then flown out to New York via Prague.

In Zimmerstrasse, a few hundred metres further on, on the right, a gateway building with the amusing name "The Wall Street Gallery" attracts attention with its decorative façade. This was once the site of the entrance to the "Markthalle III", opened in 1886 in the courtyard of the building, one of a total of 13 halls, where foodstuffs were offered for sale in the late 19th century in more hygienic conditions than on the open street markets. The market building, accessible from Zimmerstrasse and Mauerstrasse, has a notorious history. It was closed as early as 1910 because of poor sales and converted into a concert-hall called CLOU. It was here that the previously unknown Herr Hitler held his first public speech in Berlin in 1927, and where the central organ of his party, the *Völkische Beobachter*, had its offices from about 1936, as did the socialist daily paper *Neues Deutschland* in the undamaged parts of the building after the war. During the "factory operation" of 1943, SS officers gathered Jewish citizens together in the CLOU building in order to transport them to the extermination camps. (There is a commemorative plaque outside the house.) Finally, it was here that, in the winter of 1971/72, employees of the East Berlin energy company Bewag dug an escape tunnel about 21 metres long, but in vain. It was discovered before it could be used.

An operation on the next street corner that came to an end on 7 July 1977 was also unsuccessful but in a different way, since the border violator was *not* shot, but *only* arrested. He was an unemployed Pole who, according to his own testimony, had wanted to take his life.

The harsh presence of the Wall can still be discerned at numbers 6–9 Zimmerstrasse. The front of this mid-1970s dwelling-house is set back so far from the building line of Zimmerstrasse that there was room for a strip of green space with a globe Norway maple tree as a visual barrier between the house and the border. The building with its stairwells seems to be turning its back on the street.

Beyond Wilhelmstrasse, a few hundred yards of the original Wall remain – although it has been badly hacked about by souvenir-hunters, it is in fact under a preservation order. When, in the mid-1990s, the best way of marking the former route of the Wall was being considered, one idea that was tested out was a copper band along the road surface, and this is still recognisable today in the Niederkirchnerstrasse. However, this suggestion was not adopted. Niederkirchnerstrasse (known until 1951 as Prinz-Albrecht-Strasse), the former "death strip", runs between an open space and the complex of the Federal Republic's Ministry of Finance. A commemorative plaque at the entrance refers to the ominous story of the open space: in Prinz-Albrecht-Palais and in the "Kunstgewerbeschule" (School of Arts and Crafts) – which stood on what is now waste land, destroyed in the Second World War and finally cleared away between 1953 and 1963 – the Fascist terror was organised by the deskbound masterminds of the Gestapo, the SS and the Reich's Security Council, who gave orders for its execution in the underground torture chambers. The "Topografie des Terrors" (topography of the acts of terrorism) is archaeologically delineated on the site itself. An exhibition hall which has been the subject of disputes over many years is to be opened in 2005.

The building complex on the right-hand side opposite also has a Fascist past (as is pointed out by a memorial plaque on the corner of Wilhelmstrasse and Zimmerstrasse). Hermann Göring had it built in 1935/36 as the

Reich Ministry for Air Travel. One of his co-workers was Harro Schulze-Boysen, the leading light of the resistance group "Rote Kapelle", executed in 1942. An inscription in his memory can be found above one of the round windows of the extended, flat building. It was in Göring's banqueting hall that the GDR was founded in 1949, its first president was elected, and the "Volkskammer" was set up. After that, central offices and several GDR ministries moved into the "House of Ministries". After reunification in 1990 and the decision to take Berlin as the capital in 1991, the building seemed to be inadequate for the ministries of the Federal Republic. Demolition and rebuilding were considered. Then the "Treuhandanstalt" (the government body for the privatisation of former state-owned businesses) established itself there. At the end of 1994 it moved out, having disposed of the best part of the GDR's state enterprises. Since the spring of 2000, the 1,360 staff members of the Federal Ministry of Finance have been carrying out their work in the 3,000 renovated rooms.

From this site, on 28 July 1965, the Holzapfel family almost literally took flight over the Wall. The parents and their nine-year-old son hid in a toilet in the "House of Ministries" waiting for nightfall, climbed up to the roof in the dark, the father fastened a rope and threw the other end over the border strip. There a helper pulled the rope taut, and above the helmets of the baffled border guards the family dashed to safety in the West via their own home-made cableway.

Two impressive buildings had their entrances blocked by the Wall: on the left the "Martin-Gropius-Bau", Berlin's best known exhibition building, built in 1877–81 as a Museum of Arts and Crafts, and severely damaged in the Second World War. When reconstruction began in 1978, the main entrance had to be moved to the south side; only after the fall of the Wall could the original entrance be reinstated.

The main entrance of the house on the right, too, was blocked off. Here the Prussian Landtag (state parliament) met between 1899 and 1933. After that, it was used by various bodies: for a short time the "Volks-gerichtshof" (People's Court), then the nearby Reich Ministry for Air Travel ("House of Fliers") – until it was destroyed. Soon afterwards the East Berlin city council had it rebuilt. It was an important site for them, for it was here that the Communist Party of Germany had been founded at the end of 1918. After 1945 the house never found a suitable occupier. The People's and State Chambers (the lower and upper houses) never met there as originally planned, neither did the GDR's Council of Ministers, nor the council for mutual economic aid. Upon the building of the Wall, the house found itself out in the cold. Some rooms were used by the State Security Service and the 35th border regiment.

A soldier who was standing guard in front of the house was observed on 1 January 1966 as a West Berlin police officer threw something to him. A search was immediately conducted. The lockers of two border soldiers were found to contain forbidden objects – six empty packets of Western cigarettes *(Ernte 23)* and a magazine, *Stern,* came to light. The two offenders were detained for ten days.

Turning right into Stresemannstrasse, up to the end of our tour we follow the course of the Berlin city limits, as they existed from 1734 to 1861. Then, too, a wall stood here, which was also intended to prevent escape, in this case of deserters who wanted to break out of the tough Prussian military service in the Berlin garrison. The wall was razed to the ground in 1867/68, with only the Brandenburg Gate remaining.

Next to number 128, Stresemannstrasse, part of the hinterland Wall has been preserved, and behind that, an observation tower, after long controversy over demolition, preservation or conversion.

The marking strip for the Wall changes on the west side of Stresemannstrasse and is lost in Köthener Strasse in front of a house with the massive inscription "Potsdamer Platz 10". Here, up to 1972, the sector border took a confusing course. Officially the ruined space between Köthener Strasse und Linkstrasse, in particular the wasteland area of the Berlin-Potsdam railway, whose reception hall was blown up in 1958, belonged to East Berlin. But it was accessible only from West Berlin, since the border wall ignored the apparently worthless urban wasteland area. In July 1972 the Senate of West Berlin purchased the 85,000 square metres, in order to construct a connecting road. This, in turn, interrupted the U-Bahn section Gleisdreieck-Potsdamer Platz, through which no trains had passed since 1961. After reunification the street was removed, the U-Bahn connection reconstructed, and in the autumn of 1993 Potsdamer

On 13 August 1961, the Deutsche Reichsbahn, based in East Berlin, cut off eleven S-Bahn lines. It closed down 32 kilometres of track. In protest against the building of the Wall, West Berliners boycotted the S-Bahn. For 20 years the trains ran almost empty. The S-Bahn began to go into the red, and so on 9 January 1984 the Deutsche Reichsbahn handed it over to the "Berliner Verkehrsbetriebe" (BVG). However, the disrupted connections could not be restored until November 1990, and it was only in June 2002 that the S-Bahn line was ready to operate.

Two U-Bahn lines were also cut off. The BVG was able to continue using two others, which were essential for the operation of the West Berlin network, but ran below East Berlin streets. Admittedly, the trains did not stop there (except at Friedrichstrasse station). The U-Bahn entrances were removed from the East Berlin cityscape. On 1 July 1990 all the U-Bahn stations, except for Warschauer Brücke, were once more in operation.

On 29 May 1952, 200 of the 277 streets at the West Berlin border were divided, and on 13 August 1961 all the others – except for the border crossings. The local through traffic on the streets had already been abandoned before 1961, as had, in May 1952, the West sector's bus traffic to the surrounding area, on 14 January 1953 the tram routes between the two halves of the city, and in 1961 the last inner city bus routes. After 1989 the traffic connections were immediately restored. Since 1992 the BVG has also been "reunified".

DIVISION OF THE TRANSPORT SYSTEM

Platz U-Bahn station, a product of the art nouveau era, was operating once again. The underground S-Bahn (city and suburban railway) was also restored in as authentic a manner as possible. During the division of Berlin its entrances had also been blocked off, and trains passed through, without stopping, from West Berlin to West Berlin. The regional railway station was newly built.

For 14 years the "Rollheimer" (occupants of mobile homes) – the city nomads, as they call themselves – lived on the Köthener Strasse in the shadow of the Wall, "close to nature" and protective of nature, in caravans and a scrapped BVG double-decker. In 1995 they had to abandon their self-chosen niche in view of the advancing diggers and cranes. They are still trying to redesign the edges of the bulldozed Leipziger Platz, formerly in the area of the Wall. Its twin, Potsdamer Platz, has already become one of the architectural and cultural attractions of Berlin (the text on a wall on the corner of Stresemann and Potsdamer Strasse supplies further information). There is little that is authentic to encounter: Alte Potsdamer Strasse as a natural monument and Weinhaus Huth from the year 1912. The little green tower that shows the time of day is, however, only a copy of the first German traffic lights of 1924. Also, the splendidly restored, so-called "Kaisersaal" of the legendary Hotel Esplanade is no longer to be found in its original place; in 1996 it was lifted onto an air-cushion vehicle and deposited appropriately in the complex of the Sony Center.

This luxury hotel stood on Bellevuestrasse, which, together with Lenné and Ebertstrasse, forms a triangle that belonged to East Berlin, but was inaccessible from there. (The Wall ran along Ebertstrasse.) As the "Lenné triangle" the area caused a furore in the summer of 1988. The Berlin Senate bought it in order to build a motorway route. Protesting environmentalists built a village of huts here. This existed as long as the area did not belong to West Berlin and its authorities could not step in. But no sooner had the properties changed hands in

TOUR 3

the night of 1 July 1988 than police officers rushed in to arrest the occupiers. However, the latter put up ladders against the Wall and climbed into East Berlin, where they were welcomed with breakfast rolls and coffee.

On the way to the Brandenburg Gate, Ebertstrasse separates the Tiergarten from the former Wall zone. Here the "Ministergärten" extended, small park areas belonging to the Ministerial Palace in Wilhelmstrasse, the centre of government in Imperial days and during the Weimar Republic. The notorious Reich Chancellery with its "Führerbunker", parts of it still preserved but not open to the public, also stood on this site. The governments of some of the federal states have built their headquarters here.

One site, on Behrenstrasse, however has not been built up. It is intended as a site in memory of Nazi genocide. There were vehement disputes for years about this Holocaust memorial, about its justification and its monumentality, a surface with 2,700 concrete columns and an underground documentation centre (designed by Peter Eisenman). Also controversial was the building of the American Embassy on Pariser Platz, since the clients wanted the security zone to extend so far that Ebertstrasse would have had to be swept several metres away into the Tiergarten. A compromise was devised which allowed the building to take place.

The Wall ran in a wide curve around the Platz des 18. März (1959–2000: Platz vor dem Brandenburger Tor) in front of the Brandenburg Gate. The most famous architectural feature of Berlin, built as a gate of peace in 1788–91 by the architect Carl Gotthard Langhans, became a triumphal gate for Prussian-German military engagements, up to 1940. It was to be the symbol of the unity of Germany when East and West Berlin businesses restored the war-damaged gate and the quadriga in 1956–58. Instead it became the symbol of division: at 2 pm on 14 August 1961 the passage through the gate was blocked, as was officially announced, "on the grounds of continual provocation" and a "campaign of hostility carried out by representatives of the West Berlin Senate

The Reichstag building at Friedrich-Ebert-Platz (1984)

and the Bonn government" – up to 22 December 1989. On the occasions of official state visits from the West, the gate was even covered on the east side. Today, since thousands danced on the Wall and in front of the gate in November 1989, and spontaneously celebrated the arrival of New Year's Day, it has become a token of reunification.

Hardly any traces of the division are recognisable after the renovation of the gate and quadriga and the replanning of Pariser Platz, once sacrificed to an unobstructed view. On the central strip of Strasse des 17. Juni, as before, Gerhard Marcks' "Rufer" ("Caller") stands out, created in 1967, installed looking towards the east in 1989: "I go through the world calling peace, peace, peace."

The square between the Reichstag building and the former Reichstag president's palace (today the "Haus der Deutschen Parlamentarischen Gesellschaft") is called Friedrich-Ebert-Platz. When the Wall ran straight across the square on the line formed by the concrete panels inset into the ground, this was an inhospitable, usually lonely place. It is only since the first all-German "Bundestag" session on 4 October 1990, during the covering of the Reichstag" building by Christo and Jeanne-Claude in the summer of 1995, and since the German "Bundestag" (from April 1999) has been meeting here regularly, that more people have been drawn to the surroundings of the parliament building. But there were several attempts at escape in its vicinity, many with tragic outcomes.

27 April 1973: Manfred Gertzki, 30 years old, is shot in the border area before he can jump into the Spree. Border police throw the corpse into the river, where it is picked up and towed away two hours later by a boat.

26 May 1985: In the grey hours of dawn, two light aircraft, with olive-green camouflage paint and red Soviet star, land on the Platz der Republik. Three brothers climb out, breathing sighs of relief. Two of them started a good fifteen minutes earlier, in the West Berlin district of Neukölln, and flew over the border to Treptower Park. While one made a stopover landing to pick up the third, the other brother from his aircraft monitored and filmed the operation. Then they headed for the landing-strip in front of the Reichstag building, and then to the offices of a magazine, to sell their story.

6 May 1987: A 26-year-old West Berliner tries to take his own life. In his car, he races along Scheidemann-strasse, directly towards the Wall – and survives. But the car ... it smashes, demolished against the Wall, and is (because the border extends eight metres in front of it) on East Berlin land. Who is responsible for the wreck? GDR border troops, West Berlin police, British and Soviet officers, wrangle over the jurisdiction. In the end, the wreck is removed by British soldiers.

21 August 1988: Two young men, a pregnant woman and her fiancé swim across the Spree. The mother-to-be has left her three-year-old daughter behind in East Berlin with her grandmother.

14 February 1989: Three young men in a lorry break through the roadblocks on Reinhardtstrasse, leap into

the ice-cold Spree and swim for their lives. Two safely reach the opposite bank, the third is pulled out of the water by his dripping hair by the crew of a GDR border patrol boat.

17 April 1989: Two 18-year-olds have a similar experience. They enter the Spree at the Marschallbrücke and swim some 200 metres towards the south bank. One succeeds in reaching the far shore. The slower of the two is picked up by a patrol boat.

There are white crosses on Scheidemannstrasse, acting as reminders of these evil days. It is at the Spree that we end our tour.

TOUR 4

FROM SANDKRUGBRÜCKE
TO NORDBAHNHOF

Sandkrugbrücke – Kanalufer – Kieler Strasse – Boyenstrasse – Chaussee-strasse – Liesenstrasse – Gartenstrasse – Nordbahnhof S-Bahn station

Distance: 4 kilometres
Time: 2 hours

Of the 174 people who lost their lives at the Berlin Wall, who was the first to die? A stone block on the Sand-krugbrücke reminds us: Günter Litfin, 24 years old, 24 August 1961. For this day, the daily bulletin of the "Transport Police, Berlin district" just records a "breach of the state border prevented by the use of firearms". As Litfin approaches the Humboldthafen across the railway grounds, he is noticed by a double patrol of the transport police on border security duty. "Stay where you are", then two warning shots are fired into the air – well, more or less. The report continues: "The escapee did not react and proceeded towards the water via the steps down from the bank in order to swim to the Western sectors. After three machine gun shots had been fired into the water a few metres away from the escapee and he did not turn back, two direct shots were fired, upon which the man went down."

The marksmen were put on trial in 1997 at the Berlin regional court, not far from here. The principal offender received a prison sentence of eighteen months for man-slaughter, and his superior officer of a year. They showed no remorse for their action.

At the Sandkrugbrücke, the Berlin-Spandau ship canal crosses Invalidenstrasse, which was a border crossing for almost 30 years (there is information about this on the parapet of the Sandkrugbrücke). At the eastern bridgehead, piles of concrete slabs formed a zigzag roadblock. Here a failed attempt at escape took place on

12 May 1963. A BVG bus from the east with twelve passengers raced towards the border crossing, but at only 100 metres from the border it came under fire from GDR border guards. However, the driver unwaveringly continued on his way. At the last barrier the vehicle got wedged in and the passengers were arrested. (See information board.)

The checkpoint that the bus tried to break through is still able to guess who is on the traffic island keeping an eye on the entrance, still bricked up, to 88 Invalidenstrasse. On this island there was an observation roof belonging to the checkpoint. The entrances to numbers 80–83 (a radiotherapy clinic part of the Charité infirmary) and 48/49 were blocked off. Today the latter is the headquarters of the Federal Ministery for Economics and Technology. The iconography of the façade (helmets

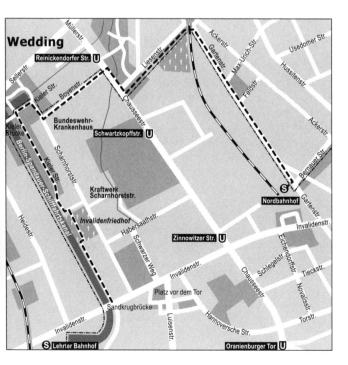

ORDER TO FIRE

In the "Politbüro Trial" from 1991 to 1997, one of the ques-
tions the Berlin regional court looked into was whether a
direct shot had been fired in escape attempts. It was a question of incitement to manslaughter, an accusation made
against several former members of the National Defence
Council. This institution, which was subordinated to the SED-
"Politbüro", the power centre of the GDR, had coordinated
and directed the defence and security measures of the GDR.
The court concluded that there had not been an "order to
fire", as it was commonly called. But when the "Politbüro"
passed on the "Klassenauftrag" ("demand of the labouring
classes") to the border troops, it had demanded the protection of the GDR border from anyone trying to escape, if
necessary, with the use of firearms and the risk that people
might be killed.

The order to "arrest or exterminate escapees", as it was called up to the 1970s, reached the border regiments from the
Defence Ministry by way of a longer chain of command. In
the end, each border soldier before his period of guard duty
was "reminded", that is, obliged, to ensure the inviolability of
the borders and to carry out his duty vigilantly and according
to the legal regulations and requirements.

Among these was the requirement that the life of the person
escaping was, if possible, to be spared. Accordingly, a border
soldier attempting to prevent the breach of a border should
conduct himself as follows: first he would call to the escapee,
demanding that he should stop. If he continued, warning shots
would follow. If these too were ignored, the soldier would try
to shoot the escapee in order to render him incapable of
flight. Lethal shots could not be excluded, as, even if only one
shot was fired, it was not possible to aim directly at the legs
with the service weapon, the Kalashnikov sub-machine gun.
And in case of doubt, the inviolability of the border was more
important than a man's life.

The GDR's border law of 1982 made special allowances for
uninvolved third parties, children, young people and women.
Their lives could in no circumstances be endangered. The
use of firearms was forbidden. However, any infringements
of this regulation were covered up by the authorities.

If an escape attempt failed, the GDR's penal code provided for a prison sentence from one to eight years for a serious case of an unlawful border crossing. The border troops could expect praise, promotion, bonuses and special leave. A successful "breach of the border" however resulted in sanctions, right up to disciplinary procedures and measures taken by the party against the company and regimental commanders. Border soldiers who refused to shoot at escapees or were observed to have deliberately shot to miss were initially temporarily suspended from service. In case of doubt as to their "ideological stability" they were transferred to office duty or to another unit.

The sentence the Berlin regional court passed on the members of the "Politbüro" still has to be mentioned. In 1997 Günter Schabowski and Günther Kleiber each received a prison sentence of three years for concomitant threefold manslaughter, and the accused Egon Krenz, a total prison sentence of six and a half years because of a further instance of manslaughter. Their appeal two years later to the Federal Supreme Court was dismissed.

Checkpoint Invalidenstrasse: "Ikarus-Bus" approaching West-Berlin (1987)

and weapons) suggest that the building was used for non-civilian purposes, and history bears this out. In 1910 Wilhelm II officially opened this impressive building as the "Kaiser-Wilhelms-Akademie", for the training of medical officers. Together with the hospital which had already been set up in 1748 for war-disabled Prussian soldiers, the park and the so-called 'Invalids' Cemetery' in Scharnhorststrasse, it formed a rather special kind of district. In 1937 the war veterans were moved to an area north of Frohnau in the district of Reinickendorf (see Tour 8: "From Frohnau to Frohnau").

After being temporarily used by the Reich Ministry of Labour (discussions took place here in 1926 about the introduction of unemployment insurance), medical officers moved into 48/49 Invalidenstrasse again in 1934. After 1949 the Ministry of Health and the Public Prosecutor's Office had their premises here, and the GDR's Supreme Court held its show trials here. More privileged members of the state and (from 1976) diplomats received medical attention in the north wing, the government hospital.

After a glance at the mosaic on the surface of the Sandkrugbrücke, a statement made in 1999 by the artist Gabriele Basch on the old border crossing, we continue along the canal, a path marked by young small-leaved lime trees. However the promenade could not be laid out until it was possible to approach the canal bank without any danger of provoking warning shots fired "more or less into the air" and "machine-gun volleys". In 1999 the avenue was laid out as a garden (see the information board).

The canal itself, which for half its width belonged to the Tiergarten district, that is, to West Berlin, was regarded at its opening in 1855 as part of a nursery garden.

The royal garden manager, Peter Joseph Lenné, had not only planned the planting of the canal bank, but had also given the waterway its sweeping contours, which, with increasing tonnage, demanded greater navigational skills by the crews of the inland ships.

For a long time, the area on the left bank of the canal officially belonged to the Deutsche Reichsbahn based in East Berlin, and was thus, although situated in West Berlin, not easily accessible. Here we find the "Hamburger Bahnhof", built in 1845–47 as a copy of the Villa Medici, one of the oldest German railway station buildings. After its closure it served as a traffic and building museum from 1906. Until 1981 on the "forbidden" grounds of the Reichsbahn, its fittings and equipment were gathering dust. Then the building became the responsibility of West Berlin. Its stock was transferred to the "Deutsche Technikmuseum", while the old railway station today houses the Museum of Contemporary Art.

The Federal Ministry for Economics and Technology on the right is, of course, dedicated to progress. The photovoltaic (solar energy) system on the roof of the long building is, at 920 square metres, one of the largest in Germany, and in bright sunshine achieves a capacity of 100 kWp. That is 76,000 kilowatt hours per year, which would cover the energy needs of about 50 households.

We enter the shady 'Invalids' Cemetery', from where so many of Prussia's heroes departed for Valhalla (see information board at the Scharnhorststrasse entrance). Frederick the Great could not know, when he had the cemetery laid out in 1748, and neither could later mourners, that this place of rest would one day be defaced by border roadblocks (which have been partially preserved). When we cross the patrol road it is hard to realise that we are walking over the foundations of a Catholic church and levelled graves (information boards on the "Topography of the Border Area" and on the "First Victim of the Wall", Günter Litfin). What has remained of the cemetery is impressive enough. Just a few steps and then we are standing in front of the lion resting at the grave of General Scharnhorst, the Prussian military reformer, who died in the Wars of Liberation in 1813. Not far from Scharnhorst we stumble on the resting-place of Hans Carl von Winterfeldt, who died for his king in the Seven Years' War in 1757. Of aesthetic interest is the tomb sculpture of Job Wilhelm von Witzleben, a work of the Royal iron foundry.

More modest is the little gravestone of the famous fighter pilot Ernst Udet, who took his own life in 1941 unable to cope with the burden of being accused of sabotage. He received a literary memorial from Carl Zuckmayer in *The Devil's General.*

"In this border district, on 23 May 1962, Peter Göring, non-commissioned officer of the 1st Border Brigade, born on 28 December 1940, in the faithful discharge of his duties to protect the state border of the German Democratic Republic, was maliciously murdered by members of the West Berlin police." This information was shown on a commemorative plaque in Scharnhorststrasse – until it was removed in 1993. What had happened?

23 May 1962: A 14-year-old boy, Walter Tews, attempts to escape. Still unobserved, he climbs the wire-netting fence at the 'Invalids' Cemetery', then the Wall. The border guards notice Walter, fire warning shots and run after him. The boy is faster, he reaches the canal, jumps and swims as fast as he can. Now the border guards aim: ten men, 121 shots. Unexpectedly, Western police return fire, and under their cover Walter reaches the opposite bank. But he has been shot by seven bullets. Though seriously injured, he is saved. On the east side, too, there is horror. A border soldier, Peter Göring, has been killed in the exchange of shots, another, Karl Laumers, is seriously wounded. Three other marksmen stand trial in May and June 2002 at the Berlin regional court, charged with attempted manslaughter of Walter Tews. They are acquitted. The proceedings against the West Berlin police officers are abandoned.

Continuing on our way, we pass the residential estate "Scharnhorsthöfe" with the last old house preserved in Kieler Strasse, at the rear of number 3, whose tenants were forced to leave in 1965. It has been restored and is occupied once again.

The former "Command Point of the GDR Border Troops" next door is a listed buiding. From here, company commanders, supported by "arrest groups", monitored the border. The tower is one of the remaining four border towers in West Berlin (see Tour 1, "From Heidelberger Strasse to the Schlesischer Busch", and Tour 8, "From Frohnau to Frohnau").

We follow the course of the canal over the restored old street profile with its kerb and the marking "Course of the Berlin Wall" inset into the pavement. Behind it there were once houses, in a good residential location by the canal. The Second World War left only two habitable houses standing, numbers 3 and 18 Kieler Strasse. Gerda Langosch, who, on 13 August 1961, saw the border being "secured" with barbed wire by so-called Spanish Riders, remembers: "In the afternoon, the bell rang at my parents' front door. It was the husband of a recently deceased friend of my mother's. Some time earlier he had moved to Berlin-Tempelhof. Out of curiosity, he had set off for my parents' house and had in fact reached it without difficulty. For fear that he might be arrested on his way back, he did not stay long. My husband accompanied him. Amazingly, he and our acquaintance arrived, unchecked, on the west side of the Boyenstrasse. At that moment, my husband realised that this was his last chance to stay in West Berlin. But because I was expecting our first child – I was five months pregnant – and I was not with him, he came back, again without being detained."

Her parents had five days' notice to move out of number 18 Kieler Strasse at the end of 1962. The border guards needed the tall building as an observation point. Later it was blown up. Today the rescue helicopters of the new hospital for the federal armed forces (former Police Hospital) land there, and again there is a sign: "Military area – authorised personnel only." There will probably never be a time without prohibitions, fences and barbed wire.

From the Kieler Brücke, built in 1883 as an iron footbridge, blocked off in 1961, restored in 1994, we gaze unconcerned at the poorly designed Nordhafen, which has always been a very peaceful area. Its tall bankside walls made the transfer of goods problematic from the start (1858). Nevertheless, right up to 1952 boats were still moored on the east bank. In 1966 things went quiet on the western side too – and became greener... Wheelbarrows were replaced by prams.

However, we will turn right to an urban ghost-town: pavements and kerbs with no road surface, horse-troughs without pumps, house entrances with no houses. Kieler Strasse was here too. And the "death strip" ran where families used to picnic under plane trees in the meadow. The path the border used to take is difficult to reconstruct today. The trail is lost in the undergrowth for a few paces, before we suddenly come upon a tarred road, on the far side of a little ditch (where the River Panke flows into the Nordhafen). The path, formerly a patrol route of the French military police, leads us around the tennis complex of the Schering sports centre around to Boyenstrasse. The Wall ran parallel to this, to the north, as can be deduced from the bushes. Boyenstrasse lay in the border area. It must have been somewhere here, as well, that two East Berlin building workers drove against the wall in a heavy lorry on 9 April 1962, and came out in the Wedding district.

From number 41 Boyenstrasse, the path of the border is once again easy to follow. Diagonally laid paving-stones in the northern parking areas show the path of the Wall. The series of paving stones curves to the right at Chausseestrasse towards the former border crossing. If it were not for the metal rabbits made by the artist Karla Sachse, inset into the road surface and pavement as a memento of the checkpoint, there really would be no reminder of this spot – except for the lonely flagpoles and noticeably tall arc lamps. The guards who observed pedestrians sat at number 94 Chausseestrasse, most of which was bricked up before it was splendidly restored in 2002.

People 'entering' in motor vehicles had to negotiate the zigzag stretch between concrete-slabs. This crossing, however, was not invincible. On 14 April 1964, five people in an armoured Opel limousine, strengthened with cement, managed to complete the distance from east to west. Two young men were not so lucky on 8 April

Parts of the hinterland wall on a cemetery near Liesenstrasse (2002)

1989. They tried to slip into West Berlin between the cars that had already been cleared – in vain. After a warning shot, they came to a halt. It was the last attempt to escape at the Berlin Wall. The two men did not need to complete their prison sentence of 20 months. On 27 October 1989, they were freed under an amnesty.

Before we continue our tour in Liesenstrasse, let us devote a few minutes to the green space on the corner of Chausseestrasse. Here we find an early example of an artistic statement with reference to the Wall, the reunification memorial by Hildegard Leest (1962). Two larger-than-life allegies of East and West, made of roughly worked shell limestone, form a symbolic bridge as they reach out their hands to each other.

In Liesenstrasse, we come to a cemetery wall in neat clinker brick. From afar, a reddish obelisk attracts our attention. We stand amazed: a German war memorial in French for the German soldiers of the French Cathedral congregation in Berlin who fell in the wars against France of 1870–71 and 1914–18. History could hardly get more complicated. A small wooden arrow indicates the most famous grave in this cemetery. A few more steps and we are standing in front of the graves of Emilie and Theodor Fontane the well-known writer.

More prominent names are close by. The cemetery of the Catholic parish of St Hedwig is the last resting place of the painter Peter von Cornelius and the hotelier Lorenz Adlon. For Bernhard Lichtenberg, the beatified Dean of St Hedwig, it was his penultimate resting place after his death in the Dachau concentration camp in 1943. Since 1965 his tomb has been in the crypt of St Hedwig.

The peace and quiet of the tomb was destroyed when the entrances to the cemeteries were blocked off in 1961 and the cemetery walls became border walls. The cemeteries were accessible only from Wöhlertstrasse, and only to relatives of the deceased in possession of a "grave card". In 1967 several reburials took place when the front part of the area was levelled off for the "death strip". At an angle to this, cemetery workers paved a path using memorial slabs. The cemetery authorities left some parts of the hinterland wall standing as a memorial and it was even 'extended' by means of a row of trees.

Once again the peace and quiet of the cemetery has been destroyed since the fall of the Wall, according to Sabine Bock, who is in charge of the cemetery: "Since the fall of the Wall, something is always going on here." Sometimes the cemetery chapel is broken into, sometimes gravestones are knocked over, sometimes a damaged tomb sculpture, sometimes wooden crosses ripped out. All just for fun.

As we get closer to the mighty, rusty railway bridge on the corner of Gartenstrasse, no longer in use since 1961, the old cemetery wall emerges from the ground, partially broken up by the roots of maple trees. Behind this there is a long section, about 15 metres, of the "border wall 75", which has been severely damaged by souvenir-hunters. Not visible to us from this point, a concrete wall about 200 metres long runs parallel to the S-Bahn tracks, set between steel girders, perhaps as a screen for the passengers of passing trains. An observation tower, BT 9, guarded the point where the patrol road passes under the S-Bahn line that crosses the sector border.

The long clinker brick wall along Gartenstrasse bordered the grounds of the Berlin-Stettin railway (Nordbahn), which from 1842 to 1965, when the ruins of the railway station were removed, had its Berlin reception building in Invalidenstrasse. After 1961 the railway wall was a welcome obstacle to escapees, additionally strengthened by a hinterland wall on the other side of the railway grounds and a wire netting fence directly behind the clinker wall.

Opposite the corner of Feldstrasse we notice a bricked-up gate. From here the "Stettin Tunnel" led under the railway grounds through to Schwartzkopffstrasse. At almost regular intervals we encounter further bricked-up entrances, until, at the corner of Bernauer Strasse, we reach the end of our tour. Today we may be puzzled by the wide crossroads; but until 1989 the number 12 bus route inevitably terminated at the turning area in front of the Wall, and it was not possible to change onto the S-Bahn. The entrance was bricked up. Today, however, the number 245 bus will take us through three former sectors back to Sandkrugbrücke.

TOUR 5

FROM NORDBAHNHOF
TO BORNHOLMER STRASSE

Nordbahnhof S-Bahn station – Bernauer Strasse – Berlin Wall Documentation Centre – Eberswalder Strasse – Wall Park – Schwedter Strasse – Behmstrassenbrücke – Norweger Strasse – Bösebrücke – Bornholmer Strasse S-Bahn station

Distance: 4 kilometres
Time: 3–4 hours (including a visit to the Documentation Centre)

The street sign opposite the Nordbahnhof S-Bahn exit, the starting point of our tour, points the way to the street where in the 1960s the Berlin Wall showed its most dreadful side. The images of houses with bricked-up windows and a church with its portal barricaded, of people jumping from windows and crawling through escape tunnels went around the world. We shall come back to these later.

In front of us is the cemetery of the Sophiengemeinde, no longer in use from 1967 onwards. In consquence exhumations, reburials and bricklaying work took place. The area behind the cemetery wall was levelled off, as a "death strip" – an absurd double meaning.

On 4 September 1962 an escape attempt failed. A man in a sailor's cap, under cover of gravestones and hedges, creeps up to the cemetery wall at the corner of Bernauer and Bergstrasse and climbs up. Shots are fired. The man falls back onto a grave mound. People rush out of Lazarus hospital opposite to help the wounded man. This is not permitted. He bleeds to death, his cap, pierced by a bullet hole, lying on the pavement. Later a stone slab is put up in memory of the "unknown victim". Not until the trial of the border marksmen did his name become known: Ernst Mundt, 40 years old (see memorial stone).

It is hard to believe that houses once stood where grass and robinias grow today, to the right and left of the old patrol road in the former border area. East Berlin ten-

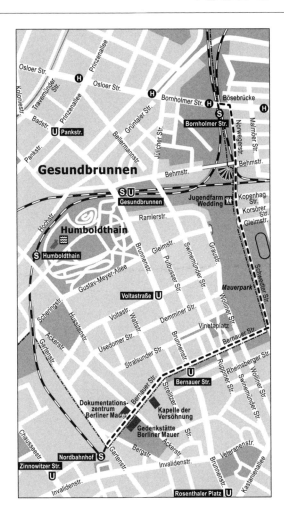

ants stepped out of their doors into West Berlin. This was no longer possible after the doors were blocked off on 19 August 1961.

But the windows were still open. In the last days of August 1961, people jumped from those windows in sheer despair, and firefighters on the pavement tried to

The premises of the "Versöhnungsgemeinde" were officially opened at number 111 Bernauer Strasse in September 1965. The church in the border area had long been out of bounds. The Documentation Centre of the Berlin Wall Association – Memorial and Documentation Centre has been housed here since November 1999 (open Wednesday to Saturday, 10 am to 5 pm, entrance free). The films, photos and documents speak for themselves. It is worth a visit. Unfortunately the financial backing for the association's work is uncertain. "We can only hope for understanding on the part of politicians," says the director, Gabriele Camphausen. The Documentation Centre is only one part of a commemorative ensemble. The "Berlin Wall Memorial", opened on 13 August 1998, is opposite. The Cologne architects Kohlhoff & Kohlhoff, who designed it, portrayed the border area over a 70-metre space, with front wall, gravel area, patrol road, lighting and hinterland wall. The steel walls, seven metres high, reflect the Wall into infinity.

The official demolition of the Berlin Wall was celebrated on Ackerstrasse on 13 June 1990. What remains of the Wall between Ackerstrasse and Bergstrasse is under a preservation order today.

The grounds of the old Church of Reconciliation are also part of the commemorative ensemble. It is actually a church like hundreds of others: red brick, Wilhelminian Gothic, consecrated in 1894. But what symbolism! On 22 August 1961, its entrance was bricked up. Then it stood idle, photographed countless times, in the border area. After an exchange of sites with the Evangelical church, the troublesome building was finally blown up in January 1985 – "in order to carry out building works for the increased security, order and cleanliness of the state border with West Berlin", as the Ministry for State Security announced. The bells, stored in the Bartholomäuskirche in Friedrichshain, were returned on the day of penance (the Wednesday 11 days before Advent) in 1995. On 9 November 2000, the community celebrated the consecration of the "Chapel of Reconciliation". The oval building with its façade of woodenslats was designed by the architects Rudolf Reitermann and Peter Sassenroth on the site of the old church.

RECONCILIATION COMMUNITY

Traces of a demolished balcony which extended into the West can still be recognised today (Schwedter Strasse, 2002)

catch them in safety blankets, unfortunately not always successfully. Rudolf Urban, 47 years old, fell to the ground on 19 August in an attempt to abseil from the first floor of his house. He died six weeks later. Ida Siekmann, 58 years old, leapt to her death on 22 August from the third floor of number 48 Bernauer Strasse. A memorial stone is inset into the pavement at the place where she fell. Olga Segler, 80 years old, of number 34 Bernauer Strasse, died as a result of her disastrous leap on 29 September.

On 21 August workers' militia groups began to clear the houses, first the ground floors, then the upper floors. Among some 2,000 people who had to leave their apartments was Regine Hildebrandt, later social services minister for Brandenburg. "My brother, my only brother," she recalled, "abseiled down from the first floor of number 10 Bernauer Strasse, with his wife, literally hanging by a string." Then the windows were bricked up.

TOUR 5

But there were still the roofs. On 4 October, two young men suddenly appeared on the roof of number 43 Bernauer Strasse. The GDR police tried to arrest them. The West Berlin police became involved. There was an exchange of fire and a GDR policeman was wounded. Finally one of the two young men was taken into custody, while the second was shot and fell to the ground. His name was Bernd Lünser.

For four years, the bricked-up row of houses presented a dreadful picture. In 1965 they were torn down, and only the ground-floor façades remained as an obstacle to flight. In the spring of 1980 these too were removed and replaced with a plain concrete wall. However, it was possible to enter some cellars secretly. Up to the early 1970s, at least 15 escape tunnels were dug, though unfortunately this was often in vain because they filled with water. One of these ran from number 55 Strelitzer Strasse, into an unoccupied bakery at number 97 Bernauer Strasse, 145 metres long and 70 centimetres high. Some Berlin students, including the later astronaut Reinhard Furrer, dug it for six months. During two nights, 2 to 4 October 1964, a total of 57 people crawled through this tunnel to the district of Wedding. Before this, however, there had been a shooting incident between helpers and border troops. One of the latter, Egon Schultz, died. Shot by the "class enemy", he became a hero of the GDR (from 1966 to 1991 Strelitzer Strasse in the Mitte district was named after him). But what the public were not told was that the lethal bullet came from a Kalashnikov. The results of the post-mortem were kept under lock and key – until recently.

Through another tunnel ("Escape tunnel 29"), 29 people crawled to the West on 14 September 1962. Then it was destroyed when a water pipe burst. A team of two Italians, two Frenchmen, one Dutchman, one US citizen and one German had spent five months digging it, from numbers 78/79 Bernauer Strasse for 120 metres, 5 metres deep, as far as number 7 Schönholzer Strasse. A team of NBC cameramen was there the whole time – for good money. The escape became a media event and all the participants profited from it – journalists, helpers and escapees.

Just as well known is the snapshot of the border guard in full uniform who jumped over a squashed-down roll of barbed wire in Ruppiner Strasse. On 15 August 1961 Peter Leibing took the picture of a lifetime. It was just a pity that he took it as a trainee on behalf of a small agency. Today he is still fighting for the copyright. Conrad Schumann, the escapee pursued by photographers and film crews, hanged himself in 1998 at his house in Kipfenberg, Upper Bavaria (see the information board).

Like Ackerstrasse, Wolgaster Strasse und Ruppiner Strasse, Swinemünder Strasse no longer leads into Bernauer Strasse from the Wedding district side, an indication that the West Berlin urban planners had taken the Wall into account. On the former corner of Swinemünder Strasse a little park was laid out.There is a memorial stone for the nine victims who died at the Wall in Bernauer Strasse.

An observation platform stood at the end of Bernauer Strasse and when the height of the Wall was increased (which happened several times), so was the platform. It was dismantled when, in the night of 11 November, 1989, a new border crossing was breached in the Wall, to the frenzied acclaim of thousands. On both the West and East sides of Berlin, even before the *Wende* (the term – literally meaning "turning-point" – is used to describe the fall of the Wall), there had been eager attempts at "turning". In the "turning circle" of Bernauer Strasse the city tour buses turned round, as did the East Berlin trams in the sharp bend at Eberswalder Strasse, trams that (as one can see from the road surface) once also passed through Bernauer Strasse.

If you are a good walker, you can climb the "mountain" (Berliners have no hills in their city!) and arrive at the top among the war rubble, before your eyes the Wedding district and the goods station of the Nordbahn, at your feet the "Wall Park" at Schwedter Strasse. The concrete Wall ran directly to the left-hand kerb, that is western kerb, of Schwedter Strasse; it has left its traces in the

road surface. When the Wall was taken down, the question arose as to what should be done with the border area. In 1993, with funds from the Munich environmental organisation, "Allianz Stiftung zum Schutz der Umwelt", the border space was turned into a green space, a "Wall Park", important for the Wedding und Prenzlauer Berg districts (see information on triangular aluminium signs).

Berlin Wall Memorial (2002)

The lack of sport and leisure areas was alleviated by the "Berliner Sportpark", today known as the "Friedrich-Ludwig-Jahn-Sportpark". It was created on the mountain of rubble directly next to the sector border for the 3rd World Festival of Youth and Students in 1951. This was one of the GDR's most prominent stadiums, where important athletics contests, Cup and Championship football matches took place – and the GDR's last international match (3 : 2 against the USA, on 28 March 1990). A few unobtrusive spectators used to sit on the west side to keep an eye, not on the ball, but on the fans, up to 35,000 of them. How quickly one or other of them might have climbed over the Wall – today adorned with graffiti – and made their way downhill to the West.

The surface of Schwedter Strasse, repaired at regular intervals where the holes for border signposts used to be, leads past the grass-covered roof of the "Max-Schmeling-Halle", built for the Olympic Games of 2000, which, contrary to the expectations of the 'Berlin city fathers', ended up being held in Sydney. We reach Gleimstrasse. The dark hole under the site of the former Nordbahn goods station, that leads to the Wedding district in the west, is called the Gleimtunnel and enjoys the privilege of an architectural monument: 130 metres long, 23 metres wide, its ceiling, repaired in 1990, supported by 38 pairs of cast iron columns. The ravages of time have clearly eaten away at it, but the structure has remained unharmed by the city traffic. It was preserved for decades – closed off with brick and wire. In the autumn of 1990 pedestrians were again permitted to enter the tunnel. On 5 October 1993 the police opened it to motorised traffic – against the expressed resistance of the people in the neighbourhood, who had become used to peace and quiet over the decades.

Schwedter Strasse (and its continuation, Norweger Strasse) belonged entirely to the border area. Even today this can be seen from their façades. The repaired road surfaces of Korsörer and Kopenhagener Strasse betray the points where the Wall turned them into cul-de-sacs. The border lighting has been transformed into civilian street lamps. But what a life it was then for the residents! Access not through their front doors (if these had not been blocked off, they would have opened onto the border area), but from the back, through the courtyards. And in the week of celebration on the 30th anniversary of the GDR in 1979, a tenant reported, there was a total curfew. Who would want to stay there? But the arrival of new neighbours caused limited pleasure: they were police officers and state security personnel, sociable and interested in others for occupational reasons!

Schwedter Steg, newly built in 1997/98, rises to Behmstrasse and to the wide bridge of the same name.

TOUR 5

The old Behmstrassenbrücke, built in 1894, has not been operational for most of its existence. Damaged in the Second World War, it could not be used again by pedestrians until after 1956 – for five years up to the building of the Wall. Since 2003, it has been used again by motor vehicles.

The tangle of railway lines seems well-nigh indecipherable. On three levels, they form a triangle between the S-Bahn stations Bornholmer Strasse (front left at the old bridge, formerly in East Berlin), Gesundbrunnen (left behind the high old bridge, formerly in West Berlin), and Schönhauser Allee (right, earlier East Berlin). These two railway stations lie on the circle line that, after the division of the city, has only completely resumed its course since June 2002.

During the division of Berlin the rails were "bent" off to the north. Bornholmer Strasse station, which was in the border area, was closed (between November 1961 and August 1991), and West Berlin trains went straight through it without stopping. The western and eastern sets of rails had long been separated by a double wall. The East Berlin trains rushed at high speed in a wide curve past Bornholmer Strasse station, over a specially created connecting track. Wherever possible without "losing" passengers, they were heading for the next station, Pankow, in the north. In the near future, long-distance trains from the north will reach the inner city of Berlin via Gesundbrunnen.

On 30 December 1952, around 8 pm (or according to West Berlin perceptions, around 10.30 pm), three shots were heard in Behmstrasse. Murder! The victim was the 19-year-old junior guard Helmut Just, shot from behind on his way to work at the sector border. The GDR police headquarters immediately identified the people behind the operation: the "rabble-rousers of the criminal general war treaty and remilitarisation" in Bonn. The young police officer was given full honours as a martyr of the GDR. Countless schools and businesses bore his name, as did Behmstrasse in Prenzlauer Berg from 1960 to 1993. The murder was never solved.

The condition of Norwegerstrasse and its houses still reveal the fact that they were once directly next to the border area. Parts of the hinterland wall are still standing. There are the spots of tar on the asphalt, showing where the concrete posts for the barbed wire barriers were placed in the road. There are bricked-up windows and doors, cleaned up and re-whitewashed to a high standard. The entrance to a former bar on the corner of Isländische Strasse no longer exists. The canalisation shaft under Behmstrasse had been forgotten, and August 1961 was a dry month. So it was down into the domain of rats, and out through the middle. For four weeks, and then, in mid-September, a grille was installed.

Our tour ends at the impressive Bösebrücke. This nickel-steel bridge, built from 1912 to 16, takes its unfriendly-sounding name (*böse* means evil or wicked) from the resistance fighter Wilhelm Böse, who was executed in 1944. It is 138 metres long; 108 metres of it belonged to East Berlin. This was where the Bornholmer Strasse border crossing was, until 1972 only to be used from the West, by those in possession of a personal identity document issued by the Federal Republic, then also the "temporary" West Berlin document. On 9 November 1989, towards 11.14 pm, the Bornholmer Brücke, as it is often wrongly called, was the first place that GDR citizens were able to travel to the West without permission. Segments of wall were falling everywhere like dominoes (memorial plaques at the taxi-rank and on the parapet of the Bösebrücke). The artist Twin Gabriel left an artistic memento there in 1999, commissioned by the city's building department. Anyone who sits down on a hard red sofa at the entrance to the S-Bahn station will hear an announcement to "mind the gap". There are many other original aspects to remind us of the border situation: the site of the command point, where a second-hand car dealer has parked his cars, the five-rayed tall lighting masts, a long strip of wall on the north side of Bornholmer Strasse, and at Björnsonstrasse the turning-place for trams (the number 52 line terminated here). The tram has only been passing over the bridge again since October 1995 – the first and, as before, the only one in West Berlin since the BVG stopped the service in 1967. But it is the S-Bahn that will now take us straight back to the starting-point of our tour at Nordbahnhof.

FROM SCHÖNHOLZ
TO MÄRKISCHES VIERTEL

Tour A: Schönholz S-Bahn station – patrol road – Wilhelmsruher Damm
Tour B: Schönholz S-Bahn station – border area or patrol road –
Hertzstrasse – Fontanestrasse – patrol road – Wilhelmsruher Damm

Distance: 6–7 kilometres
Time: 2 hours

This is a tour for technology and railway enthusiasts. The starting point is a railway station. A nostalgic shiver is evoked by the words "Berlin-Schönholz" on the enamel signs and the red and yellow clinker-brick platform buildings, some 120 years old, with their iron and timber construction and rounded-off corners. Schönholz station was where the tracks of the Nordbahn to Neubrandenburg, opened in 1877, met the Kremmener Bahn and the popular Niederbarnimer railway line (the "Heidekrautbahn" or "Heather Railway") to Groß-Schönebeck. The arrival of one of the trains was filmed in 1896 by the Skladanowsky brothers, Germany's first film-makers. The film was so realistic that the audience panicked as they thought they were being run over by the train. Day-trippers from Schorfheide met in Schönholz and changed onto the Nordbahn, the S-Bahn or the tram. In between they would enjoy a glass of brandy. But not that much brandy was actually consumed – most of it was shunted on the 1,700-metre track to Schönholz goods station. This connection belonged to the monopoly administration for brandy, established in Provinzstrasse in 1919.

The Niederbarnimer railway was taken over by Deutsche Reichsbahn on 1 July 1959. Nevertheless the business was still based in West Berlin. Until 9 November 1961 the Heidekrautbahn continued to run as far as Wilhelmsruh, the next station to Schönholz to the northwest. Then the terminus station was returned to GDR territory, to Schildow, and later removed to Berlin's Karow district. Since 1991 the Niederbarnimer railway company has resumed responsibility for the line and has invested in the Heidekrautbahn. But nobody knows – not even the politicians concerned – if the trains will ever go further than Schönholz again. Leaving the station, so full of memories, we turn right and find ourselves in Provinzstrasse. A few metres from here, at the Strasse vor Schönholz, where once cars, etc rushed along close to the border area, demolition work on the Berlin Wall was officially completed on 30 November 1990. But after the excavators' last few trips had been photographed, the Wall was gone. In the meantime, Provinzstrasse had already been repaired under the railway line. The "vordere Sperrelement" (front blocking element), that is the Wall that was visible from the West, ran directly under the

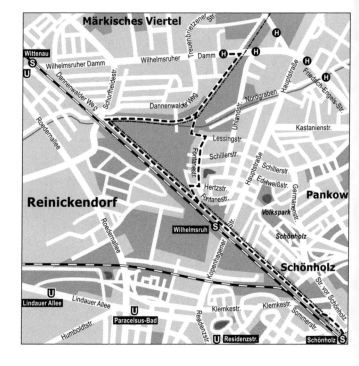

Approach to the border area at Kopenhagener Strasse (1984) S-Bahn bridge. A double row of paving stones right across the street marks where it used to be. There was a wide border area behind the front blocking element, and today this is still as uncultivated as it was then. In the border area, alsations ran to and fro in their enclosures, and the traffic route nearby, today "Cycle Path 11" to Glienicke, had been asphalted for the border patrol.

We will take this route as far as the bridges over Klemkestrasse. The tracks of the Kremmener Bahn, branching off to the left towards Tegel and Hennigsdorf, separate from those of the Nordbahn here. Since 1995 the S-Bahn has been running to Tegel again, and since 1998 also beyond the city limits to Hennigsdorf. East and West joined forces to restore Klemkestrasse – with street lamps: on the east concrete masts, on the west the more modern-looking green candelabra. The lamps still cast light on where the "east" and "west" used to be.

We will head for the "west". A modest crucifix commemorates Horst Frank, the 20-year-old border soldier, shot while trying to escape on 29 April 1962.

TOUR 6

Before reaching the bridges, we take the asphalt path to the right. The Allies' military police and their West Berlin colleagues used to carry out their tours of inspection on this route. We can either take this path to the next street or struggle through the narrow overgrown footpath in the former border area. Both routes lead back again to the patrol road just in front of Kopenhagener Strasse.

A mysterious event took place there on 16 March 1981. For unknown reasons, a man of about 40 climbed over the Wall from a West Berlin observation platform and ran through the border area. Border troops at a nearby watch tower saw him, fired warning shots first and then direct shots, two of which hit and killed him.

VEB (STATE-OWNED ENTERPRISE) BERGMANN-BORSIG

In 1891 Sigmund Bergmann founded the electrical engineering firm S. Bergmann und Co. in Berlin, and in 1900 he merged it with his electric motor and dynamo factories to create "Bergmann-Elektricitäts-Werke AG". In 1909 the business opened in Wilhelmsruh. Before and during the Second World War, Bergmann was an important arms factory. Then it was destroyed, dismantled, rebuilt and – expropriated. Publicly owned since 1949, the business was called "Bergmann-Borsig", a misleading name, since "Borsig AG" continued in business in West Berlin's Tegel district. The state-owned enterprise (VEB) Bergmann-Borsig became the permanent Berlin base of the "Kraftanlagenbau" combine. Its gas and steam turbines for power stations were some of the GDR's top-class products. The staff were particularly active at the time of reunification in 1989. It was no use. In 1990 the "Treuhandanstalt" (privatisation body) took over the business and sold it to ABB the following year. The 3,400 employees were reduced to 400, and various parts of the concern were hived off. At the end of 1998 ABB moved the steam power-station branch to Mannheim and practically closed down the Wilhelmsruhe works. That site was redesignated as an area for service and trade offices. Meanwhile, 80 businesses with some 1,800 employees now work at the PankowPark site.

How different it was in the same place almost four years later, on 21 February, for a little black cocker spaniel! He too jumped from the observation point into the border area. The dog got stuck in a crack in the Wall and could not find his way back. Soon a crane approached from the Pankow side. A border soldier abseiled down and rescued the spaniel. Eight hours of effort paid off, and the little four-legged 'border provocateur' was saved. Four years before the 'border 'provocateur' had only been given a few minutes. For a few days the dog was the star of the Berlin popular press. They called him "Pinky", an allusion to the rock group Pink Floyd and their song "The Wall".

South of the S-Bahn bridge, at Wilhelmsruh S-Bahn station, we can see the turning-place for the number 71 buses, which used to terminate at the Wall.

After a few metres on Cycle Path 11, we can choose between two versions of the tour, Tour A (about 2 kilometres) and Tour B, which is half as long.

TOUR A:

Following the traffic route, we pass by a group of allotments (the Heidekrautbahn used to turn off to the right here) and the former site of the Bergmann-Borsig works.

Over a length of 2,000 metres the Bergmann-Borsig company area was surrounded on all sides by a high wall – even on its east side, the former track of the Heidekrautbahn. Employees had to show their passes at the factory gates. There was no metal lattice fence, only the concrete wall. The border area extended narrowly between the wall and the factory buildings, whose doors, gates and windows were bricked up or barred, as one can still see. A section of hinterland wall, some 15 metres long, is still standing. The lamps fixed to the outside of the buildings illuminated the border at night.

At the Nordgraben, which the Berlin city council had built between 1928 and 1938 for the city drainage system to draw off rainwater, the patrol road turns off to the right. Rainwater from heavy downpours can be diverted from the small river to the larger Havel through the conduit which connects Tegeler See with the River Panke.

Our route runs parallel to Dannenwalder Weg at the edge of the district known as Märkisches Viertel. Between 1963 and 1974, more than 17,000 apartments were built here on the sites of former allotments. They offered housing for 50,000 people, with the necessary infrastructure: eight primary schools, two comprehensive schools and 15 day nurseries.

After about 800 metres our route turns off to the left. Tours A and B meet up again here.

TOUR B:

After a few metres of the patrol road, a narrow footpath branches off to the wasteland site of the former border area. We will follow this in a north-westerly direction. The path brings us to an asphalted road, the old patrol road, still in use. The border solders drove into the border area from Hertzstrasse here. Lamps on tall concrete posts bathed the road in bright light. They have become unnecessary. Factory buildings belonging to the former state-owned Bergmann-Borsig company, are on the left. They are now listed buildings (for the history of the company, see page 78). The windows, facing the border area, are still barred today. Marks in the surface of Hertzstrasse show where the entrance gates to the border area used to be.

From the historic works entrance built in 1909, we leave behind the section of hinterland wall that used to continue straight on from here. We turn right into Hertzstrasse, then left into Fontanestrasse, where the sidestreets all ended up as cul-de-sacs at the border of the factory site and where the hinterland wall also stood. We can still see part of it in Schillerstrasse.

PankowPark, the former site of Bergmann-Borsig's premises, is reached from Lessingstrasse. A small memorial to the Wall on the site reminds us of how the site was completely sealed off from its surroundings for 2,000 metres.

Border zone
on the former
site of Bermann-
Borsig, today
PankowPark
(2002)

Cars are parked on an open area directly in front of the entrance. A narrow footpath behind this leads directly across the former border and over the tracks of the old Heidekrautbahn back to the asphalted patrol road. Tours A and B meet up again here.

The tracks that run parallel to the road here were rebuilt on the former Wall area. They were used to gain access to the site of the ABB factory, the successor to Bergmann-Borsig. The overgrown right-hand side of the patrol road and the waste land behind it still show us where the Wall used to be.

The border area cut through part of the state-owned cemetery no. VII. The area has been returned to the cemetery and grassed over. Burials are held here again. Members of the "Volkssturm", the German territorial army, who fell in the last months of the war are buried in a special military section of the cemetery. Their dates of birth and death make one pause for thought. Here are 15-year-old children and 77-year-old men, forced to die for "Führer" and "Vaterland", when nothing more was to be gained by battle.

Our tour ends at the Wilhelmsruher Damm bus stop where the buses used to turn off in front of the Wall. Today there is no reason to do so. We board the 122 bus and travel to the right across the "border", back to Wilhelmsruh S-Bahn station, from where we can take the S-Bahn to Schönholz.

FROM GLIENICKE TO LÜBARS

Tour A (on foot): Glienicke (Church) – Hauptstrasse – Oranienburger
Chaussee – Veltheimstrasse – Amandastrasse – Karl-Marx-Strasse –
Alte Schildower Strasse (right) – Veltheimstrasse – "Wanderweg: Lübars,
Dorfanger" (white square with red stripe) – Barnimer Dörferweg – Alt-Lübars

Distance: 5 kilometres
Time: 1.5 hours

Version B (on foot or by bicylcle): Glienicke (Church) – Hauptstrasse –
Oranienburger Chaussee – Veltheimstrasse – Amandastrasse –
Karl-Marx-Strasse – Alte Schildower Strasse (left) – Kurze Strasse –
former patrol road – Bahnhofstrasse – Blankenfelder Chaussee – Alt-Lübars

Distance: 8.5 kilometres
Time: 2.5 hours (on foot), 1 hour (by bicycle)

The Glienicke (Kirche) bus stop is the starting point of
this tour: a few metres along Hauptstrasse, and then we
turn left into Oranienburger Chaussee. The border ran
along what is now a busy street, and the east and west
walls were along the two pavements. The actual border
area was comparatively narrow, 15 to 20 metres wide,
and supposedly easy to get across. 25-year-old Michael
Bittner's escape attempt on 24 November 1986 ended
in death when he was shot by border troops not far from
here.

The course of the city border in this area is peculiar.
The whole of Oranienburger Chaussee (road number 96)
belongs to the province of Brandenburg, thus, until 1990,
to the GDR district of Potsdam. Through traffic in the
northernmost part of the Frohnau district of Berlin had
to be completely diverted, since road 96 was no longer
accessible after 1961. But the territorial situation was
even more confusing where Am Sandkrug and Falken-
weg branch off to the west. These two streets belonged

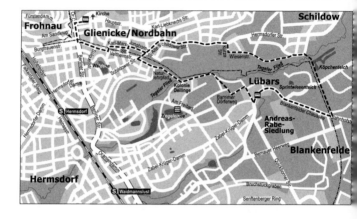

to the Potsdam district, as did the neighbouring built-up areas. On city maps, this corner of the area, about 150 metres wide and half a kilometre long, looks as if it projects into Frohnau in the shape of a duck's beak – and that gave it its nickname. The narrow "Entenschnabel" (duck's beak) was 'strangled' on all sides by high fences, border areas and walls. On the right of number 43 Oranienburger Chaussee, an overgrown little "meadow" hints at the course of the wall, which curved off to the right here.

Even today, anyone who goes about 300 metres along the street called Am Sandkrug feels the isolation which the oppressive Wall created. Some of the striking features are the tall lamp-posts, the wooden power masts with their insulators, the cables which have now been disconnected and the vegetation that has spontaneously sprung up behind the gardens of the houses since the border area disappeared. And in the middle of Silvesterweg, which is still impassable, there is a warning sign put up by the Reinickendorf council: "No dumping of rubbish".

Right in front of the sign for the city of Berlin, the border area crossed the Oranienburger Chaussee. The path cut through the forest by the border can easily be seen on both sides of the street. On 3 March 1990 the residents organised a party to celebrate the opening of the "duck's beak" and the fact that cars could once again use the road – only open to cyclists and pedestrians until the road surface had been repaired.

The road, where the border soldiers used to go on patrol, has returned to its natural state since the demolition of the border installations. It is no longer possible to walk or cycle along here. Our tour therefore now goes parallel to the former section of the Wall and then turns left into Veltheimstrasse in the Hermsdorf district. From their terraces, the owners of the properties to the left looked out onto a strangely high garden wall which they hadn't built themselves. Not far from here, in 1899, an enterprising local carpenter had drilling work carried out for a salt-water spring. From a depth of 320 metres, warm salt water (18 degrees) came gushing out at a rate of 54 litres an hour. The spring, named "Kaiserin-Auguste-Viktoria-Quelle", was furnished with a pump-room, but no clientele worth mentioning ever materialised. The dream of a health resort was not so easily given up. Hermsdorf competed with a Kneipp cure spa – but this too failed to flourish. Solquellstrasse (Salt-water Spring Street), the first side-street, is a reminder of those modest hopes of the past.

The third side-street, Amandastrasse, leads out of Berlin to the left, via the former border area, which gradually becomes more and more built up, to Karl-Marx-Strasse in Glienicke, on the other side of the border. On the right, slender concrete posts, studded with rusty remains of fencing, show what is left of the hinterland blocks.

Jungbornstrasse (the continuation of Karl-Marx-Strasse) crosses Alte Schildower Strasse. Turning off to the right, we return to Berlin-Hermsdorf (Tour A).

To the left, Alte Schildower Strasse continues for another kilometre or more into the former patrol road of the border area (Tour B [see page 88]).

TOUR 7

TOUR A:

The road surface of Schildower Strasse suddenly dete-
riorates as it enters Berlin revealing where the world was
once 'boarded up'. Veltheimstrasse comes to an end
after about 400 metres to the left. There is a path towards "Lübars, Dorfanger" (white square with red stripe)
in the valley of the Tegel river.

The Fließ, a little river meandering in a leisurely fash-
ion, forms a marshy area at Lübars before it flows into
the Havel at Tegel. About 260 hectares of the Fließ valley
has been a nature reserve since 1941, because the area
is so rich in rare plant and animal species, including
eleven species of amphibians and reptiles as well as 75
of breeding birds It is also part of the European nature
reserve system "Natura 2000".

Notices along the nature trail, which leads over wooden
planks across the marshy soil, only explain a few of the
plant and animal species that are so highly valued for
their rarity.

On the left, that is north of the footpath, the border between Berlin and the GDR ran along the northern bank

The Wall at
Blankenfelder
Chaussee
(1984)

of the marshy Fließ. However, the ground was only firm enough to support a concrete wall about 100 metres north of this. And so the wall was built away from the river, and could hardly be seen from the Fließ valley.

The footpath is part of "Barnimer Dörferweg", which goes from the Fließ at Tegel via Lübars, Karow and Ahrensfelde to the Wuhletal and leads into the 32-square-kilometre recreation area "Berliner Barnim" with a wonderful view of the surrounding area.

As soon as Lübars comes into view, the character of the landscape changes. Water meadows and pastures hint that a village is nearby. "Barnimer Dörferweg", part of which is a bridle-path, leads between paddocks directly to the village green.

Lübars is something special. As far as we know from its history, handed down since 1247, events of any great importance have bypassed the village. It was so far off the beaten track that it was of no interest to the strategists of war. Even the Thirty Years War, which depopulated whole tracts of land, had no effect on the village. Shortly before the end of the Second World War there were two fires – otherwise peace reigned here. Even the Wall, which was hardly visible, made a wide detour around the village in the most north-easterly corner of West Berlin.

Lübars – a place of relaxation. If the walled-in West Berliners felt like taking it easy at the weekend rather than departing for "West Germany" on the "interzone route", they were – until the implementation of the Four Powers Agreement and the Basic Treaty between the Federal Republic and the GDR in 1972 – dependent on such places as Lübars. Many Berlin kids saw real horses here for the first time, and were able to sniff some real country air. Their parents enjoyed the serenity and cosiness of the museum-like village in the shadow of the village church of 1793, or took refreshments in the inn, the Alter Dorfkrug. And here, where the 222 bus terminates, our tour also ends.

TOUR 7

TOUR B:

Schildower Strasse with its many bends narrows after about one kilometre, and from this point it was tarmacked for the vehicles of the border troops. With this patrol road, without ever realising it, they created a superb cycle path for the time after reunification, which is often used at weekends. On the right it passes Eichwerder, whose marshy meadows are part of a nature reserve area.

Kurze ("short") Strasse branches off to the left soon after the sign for "Schildow Landkreis Oberhavel". A private housing estate has been built here in recent years. The owners of number 8a, at the end of the street that really is as short as its name suggests use part of the old border fence as their garden fence.

From Kurze Strasse we turn left again onto the patrol road, built with its laybys through dry meadows. The dune-like terrain offered the border soldiers good visibility. Following the course of the border, the patrol road, turns south after some 1,300 metres. At this point there was – and still is – access from the northerly village of Schildow.

In a southerly direction, the patrol road crosses the Fließ to the boundary of Blankenfelde, and once again we are on Berlin soil. Leaving Kölpchensee and a meadow with fruit trees on the left, the path rises steeply with a view of Schildow in the background.

At the top of the hill, Bahnhofstrasse (on the Lübars side called Blankenfelder Chaussee), crosses the road linking Blankenfeld and its western neighbouring village, Lübars. A few steps to the right, and we have reached the former line of the Wall (the avenue leads to Lübars, the final point of the tour).

A commemorative stone is hidden next to the street sign "Bahnhofstrasse". A plaque has been screwed to an original piece of wall, recalling a "courageous breach of the border" that took place on 16 June 1990. The whole thing has a decidedly humorous background. Everywhere in Berlin, in the middle of June 1990, the Wall was being torn down. The border was hardly guarded any more for the last two weeks before its legal abolition, when the treaty regarding the currency, economic and social union of the two German states came into effect. But in Lübars, where time seemed to stand still, the Wall was still standing just as before. Then the Lübars farmer Helmut Qualitz had the idea of putting the concrete blocks that stood on Blankenfelder Chaussee "to one side" and opening the road again. No sooner said than done. Qualitz drove his tractor out of the garage, fitted a front loader, hit the accelerator and crashed through the wall. With his son and a friend he pushed the concrete rubble to one side. Next day, he paid a visit to the astonished volunteer fire brigade in Blankenfelde. The firefighters lent a hand, and when all the remains of the Wall had been removed, they consumed a case of champagne. "Of course I'm pleased about the plaque," said Qualitz at the unveiling ceremony. "But I don't see what was so brave about what I did."

TOUR 8

FROM FROHNAU TO FROHNAU

Frohnau S-Bahn station – Ludolfingerplatz – Maximiliankorso – Gralsburg-steig – Border area – Staehleweg – Invalidensiedlung – Florastrasse – Berliner Strasse – Gewerbestrasse – Border area – forest paths – Geierpfad – Schwarzkittelweg – Bieselheider Weg – Schönfließer Strasse – Zeltinger Strasse – Zeltinger Platz – Frohnau S-Bahn station

Distance: 13 kilometres
Time: 4 hours

Historians do not usually hypothesise, but just for once let's do it! If the landowner Werner von Veltheim had not sold the best part of Stolper Heide to Guido Graf Henckel Fürst von Donnersmarck and his Berlin Terrain-Centrale in 1907; if this property company had not laid out the garden city or, more precisely, the villa suburb of Frohnau on this site, and if the 1,191 residents of Frohnau had not agreed to be incorporated into the city of Greater Berlin in 1920, we would not have needed to undertake today's tour of the Wall. There would have been no walls or border fences here, for Frohnau would not have be-longed to the West Berlin district of Reinickendorf, but to the GDR's district of Oranienburg. In addition, in 1937 a certain Burghard von Veltheim sold the Stolpe prop-erty to Berlin. For eight years, the capital of the Reich managed the farm, formerly privately run, as an estate of the city. Then complications arose – one after the other.

We begin our tour at the junction of three streets, Gralsburgsteig, Neubrücker and Schönfließer Strasse, a fifteen-minute walk from Frohnau S-Bahn station (via Ludolfingerplatz and Maximiliankorso). The "west" wall, that is the so-called "vordere Sperrelement" (front block-ing element), bordered directly on the north side of Schönfließer and Neubrücker Strasse. Crossing these, we reach a footpath in the former border area, which nature is gradually taking over. If we keep well to the left of the narrow sandy path that winds its way through the heathland, after about 300 metres we will reach a

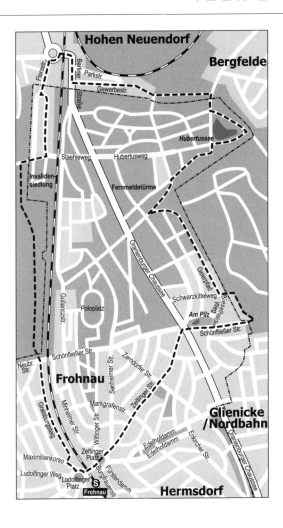

tarmac road, the old patrol road, where the GDR border troops undertook regular observation patrols along their state border. We will turn to the right.

According to the land register, our path goes as far as the land boundary mark of Stolpe, which we imagine, rather than see, on the horizon about two and a half kilometres to our left. This Stolpe estate gave rise to all sorts of complications in the early postwar years. The property of Berlin, it belonged to the Soviet-occupied zone at first. But on 10 November 1945 the Soviet military administration handed over the 615 hectares to their French colleagues, who wanted to build an airfield here. By the end of 1948 not a single digger had moved, on the contrary: runways for the airlift had been built in Tegel, also French-occupied, and the city's most important airport is now located here.

With the blockade of Berlin in that ice-cold winter of 1948/49, the Cold War was in its most heated phase: on 16 December the French city commandant in Tegel ordered a radio mast of the East Berlin radio station to be blown up. Two days later the Soviet military administration informed him that the cession of Stolpe was over. And on 21 December Soviet soldiers occupied the village again. This was explicitly deplored by the West Berlin city council, but legally nothing could be done. Stolpe was back in the Soviet-occupied zone.

Somewhere between Stolpe and the Frohnau of today (no one knows exactly where) there was once a village, a wasteland as early as the 14th century: Zerndorf. Around 1800 there had been a farm of the same name, but this too has disappeared. However, the precise date of its disappearance is known: 31 May 1945. The war had been over for a few weeks, but a goods train carrying left-over ammunition was still standing on the tracks of the Nordbahn in Berlin-Hermsdorf. A railway worker realised the danger, with great spirit organised a locomotive and bravely pulled the carriages with their high-explosive load out of the town to a part of the line between stations. There the train exploded and with it Zerndorf. It was never rebuilt. However, there is still a Zerndorfer Weg. Before the border was blocked off in 1952 Zerndorfer Weg connected Stolpe, Frohnau and Glienicke, but today it is no longer a through road. The bridge where Zerndorfer Weg crossed under the Nordbahn, is still there (we will pass it), but the road itself at this point is no more than a sandy path.

The red scaffolding of the telecommunications mast towers above the railway embankment, where we hear rather than see the S-Bahn train rush past from Frohnau to Hohen-Neuendorf. At 358 metres the mast is somewhat lower than its more famous big brother at Alexanderplatz. Since 1979 the directional aerial of the Frohnau mast transmitted the telephone connection from the walled-in half of the city to Gartow an der Elbe in Lower Saxony, 133 kilometres away.

After about 800 meters the patrol road ends at the sign: "Restaurant Hubertus-Baude 50 m". Let us head towards it and enjoy the individual atmosphere of the "Invalidensiedlung".

Captain Wilhelm Staehle, after whom the access road to the "Invalidensiedlung" is named, was its only commandant – a soldier of the old school. As a 23-year-old in 1900 he had been a member of the German expeditionary force against the Chinese Boxer Rising ("Germans to the front!") and had returned much decorated

THE "INVALIDEN-SIEDLUNG"

In 1748 Frederick II of Prussia opened a "hospital for injured soldiers" in front of the walls of Berlin (see Tour 4: From Sandkrugbrücke to Nordbahnhof). Until 1918 this home for the disabled was a regular unit of the Prussian army. This meant that the war-disabled inmates were still liable for compulsory service, received pay, wore uniform and were answerable to a commandant. As a result of the disarmament decisions of the Treaty of Versailles, the home was transformed into a foundation, but in 1937 the "Wehrmacht" took possession of the house and handed it over to the medical officers' academy for their use. The severely injured frontline soldiers had to move out, but were given a new home, adapted for disabled people, between Frohnau and Hohen-Neuendorf; the 51 houses of the "Invalidensiedlung" were ready for occupation by 1939. Today, the "Invalidenhaus" foundation has been revived and is managed by the Department of Health and Social Services. Since 1981, apartments have also been rented to people whose handicaps are not the result of a world war.

from the First World War. After that he worked at the Army Ministry and in the benefits department of the "Wehrmacht". In 1937 Staehle took over the command of the "Invalidenhaus". A conservative, he was never able to come to terms with National Socialism. Together with his wife Hildegard, he sheltered victims of persecution in his government apartment and got into contact with the conservative resistance group led by Carl Goerdeler. After Hitler's murder, Staehle was to lead the retreat of the "Wehrmacht" from the Netherlands and Belgium. However, the assassination attempt failed on 20 July 1944, Staehle was taken into custody and shot dead just before the end of the war, on 22 April 1945. His wife found his body and had him buried in the Invalids' cemetery. Hildegard Staehle, no less courageous than her husband, was imprisoned in Ravensbrück concentration camp. She was one of the co-founders of the CDU (Christian Democratic Party) in Berlin. A few months after her husband's death, she was killed in a car accident.

Back to the present day. The half-overgrown inn sign "Hubertus-Klause" attracts our attention to the former community house of the "Invalidensiedlung" with its beautiful terrace. On Sunday afternoons tea-dances are held here, primarily for the 'more mature' ladies. For some time now, widows have been allowed to stay on in these familiar surroundings after their husbands' death.

Behind the "Hubertus-Klause" we turn left into the former Eberhardstrasse. The Dutch-looking houses seem to be presenting themselves for inspection with alternate eaves and gables. The pediments of the house entrances serve as a reminder of Prussia's glory. We casually inspect the parade of houses, and leave the parade ground of military social life behind house number 1 between the little gatehouses above Florastrasse. A few remaining parts of the hinterland wall (number 7 Florastrasse) show that the zone border once ran along here. The old border area on both sides of Florastrasse is still easily recognisable too. The railway embankment on our right was taken into the border area in order to get a better view. The S-Bahn connection between Hohen-Neuendorf and Frohnau had been cut off since 13 August 1961. Frohnau station was the terminus on the West Berlin side until, on 31 May 1992, the rails were linked up again. On the other side of the border, the Reichsbahn installed a connecting piece of track to enable the trains to go right round the city area of West Berlin. It came into operation on 19 November 1961.

The railway embankment forces us to make a brief detour, before we reach the border area again: we have to go on as far as the roundabout, turn right into Berliner Strasse, under the railway bridge, and then left opposite the petrol station into Gewerbestrasse.

It leads into the trading estate that has grown out of the old border area. At the end of Gewerbestrasse, a footpath and cycle-path at the corner of Parkstrasse (in the direction of "Naturschutzturm") takes us down into the wood. Walking between recently planted oak trees, we encounter the old patrol road again which we follow to the left, until – rubbing our eyes in surprise – we are standing in front of a whitewashed, bright white tower, for the protection of the countryside. Once it protected the border from escapees – one of four remaining watch towers at the border to West Berlin (see also Tour 4, From Sandkrugbrücke to Nordbahnhof, as well as Tour 1, From Heidelberger Strasse to the Schlesischer Busch). The name "Naturschutzturm" (nature conservation tower) and the emblem of the "Deutsche Waldjugend" (German Forest Youth) cause some confusion.

Let us explain. On both sides of the border in Hohen-Neuendorf and Frohnau, even before 1989, there were youth groups who spent their free time doing conservation work. The "Ökokellerkinder" or "Ökokekis" (eco-kids) met in the cellar of a house in Hohen-Neuendorf, while the Frohnau "Brummbären" (growling bears) of the "Deutsche Waldjugend" took care of their forest. The "Ökokekis" got into serious trouble in 1990, when the former owners filed a claim for their headquarters in Hohen-Neuendorf. But they knew what to do. They contacted the border regiment in Strausberg which was responsible, bought the tower and a further 4,000 square

TOUR 8

metres of border land for a few GDR-marks. Some people who 'belonged together' actually grew closer after
the fall of the Wall, as did the conservationists in East
and West. And so the young people of Hohen-Neuendorf and Frohnau manage the building collectively, as
"Deutsche Waldjugend – Naturschutzturm Berliner
Nordrand e. V." (an exhibition on the history of the tower
is open every Friday afternoon).

The former
watch tower:
now a nature
conservation
tower (Hohen
Neuendorf,
2002)

Passing the tower, we continue our walk along the former patrol road, until this ends at another reforested part
of the border area. The path that was cut through the forest for the border can be clearly recognised in spite of
the young plants which are growing here.

It was presumably this section of the border that two
men succeeded in breaking through at 3.40 am on
22 November 1980. 18-year-old Marinetta Jirkowski's
escape attempt, however, ended in her death. It was
recorded in correct official language in the daily bulletin,
number 372, 328/80: "The female escapee, together
with two other, male persons, had mounted the GSZ

["Grenzsignalzaun" or border signal fence] with the help
of a ladder, and set off the alarm in doing so. When the
female escapee was observed at the level of the patrol
road, the guards on duty fired warning and then direct
shots, wounding J. by a shot in the stomach. [...] She died
as a result of the wound at about 11.30 pm on 22.11.1980
in the KKH ["Kreiskrankenhaus" or district hospital],
Hennigsdorf."

The path to the right is paved with small stones. We
pass some white poles, and we have changed sides. We
are now "in the West". A few more steps, a crossroads,
and we enter the patrol road to the right, laid out with
large paving stones, on which the French military police
and their West Berlin colleagues conducted their patrols.
It leads us around Hubertussee, which shimmers through
the trees to the right. This pond and its marshy bank have
been a nature reserve since 1959. The area was created
when the garden town of Frohnau was laid out. This was
where the soil came from that was used at Frohnau station to build Zeltinger and Ludolfingerplatz.

After a wide curve to the left which is hardly noticeable,
we reach a point at which a small bridge over a ditch
leads to the former border area. But we will keep to the
right on the "Wanderweg (ramblers' footpath) 1". However, anyone who is persistent enough to beat a path to
the side through the bushes will come across a little path
which a ramblers' guide issued an urgent warning about
as long ago as 1968: "The somewhat upward-sloping
road that turns off more sharply to the left is not to be
recommended, since it runs too closely along the zone
border." But it is precisely here that there is still much to
be seen of the zone border. We come across crumbling
concrete posts. Many trees bear the deep scars of the
border fences that were nailed firmly to them. And there
are even remains of rusty barbed wire stuck in the bark
of some of the trees.

Immediately next to a small hut to protect people from
the rain there is a crossroads, where a stone is marked
with the next part of "Wanderweg 1": "Geierpfad" (Vulture
Path). We walk along this path, which can be seen clearly

through the trees to the left of the sandy border area, until we come out at the end of "Geierpfad" into the estate at the edge of the forest. Turning left at Schwarzkittelweg into Bieselheider Weg, and crossing the latter, we find ourselves standing in the old border area again. To the right, we reach Schönfließer Strasse.

It was close nearby that on 12 November 1986, about 10.30 pm, 20-year-old Peter Richter and his friend Andreas Kunze, five years older, made a successful escape attempt. It took four minutes of suspense. They creep into the cordoned area. Lean the ladder they have brought with them against the first wall, two and a half metres high. Pull up the ladder. Climb over. Jump into the raked border area. Carry the ladder through the area, taking care to avoid the tripwires (which could set off the alarm). Lean the ladder against the western wall. Climb up – but now they have given themselves away. Shots ring out. The two young men jump down from the top of the wall and run for it. They reach Bulgenbachweg. Breathlessly, they ring a doorbell. The door is opened. They have done it.

We may wish to end our tour here as well. Back to Frohnau station via Schönfließer Strasse, passing the "Pilz", and Zeltinger Strasse.

But anyone who is not completely exhausted by this walk can follow us along Oranienburger Chaussee on a detour to Edelhofdamm. Here, we are touched by a modest memorial, a cross in front of a section of wall with the inscription "In memory of the victims of the Berlin Wall 13. 8.1961 – 9.11.1989". It is dedicated in particular to Herbert Bauer and Michael Bittner, who died here in 1952 and 1986.

Michael Bittner's escape attempt was especially tragic. What do we mean by "tragic"? The 25-year-old bricklayer could stand it no longer in the GDR. He already had short prison terms on his record when he decided to escape. "What will you do with yourself over there, all alone?" his mother asked. "But he remained stubborn." On 24 November, when she returned from work, her son had gone. "Next day one of my colleagues said to me: 'Have you heard? They've shot another one dead in

Frohnau!' That made my heart sink into my boots." What she did not know was that Michael had succeeded in crossing the border area. But at the Western wall, continuous firing started. The shots, from 160 to 180 metres, hit their mark. Today Michael's mother still does not know where her son's body was taken.

Witnesses reported, one of the two marksmen went to pieces after this event. He tore his cap from his head, banged his hand against his forehead several times and shouted repeatedly, "Scheiße, Scheiße". The young man was disarmed and taken away.

On 27 November 1997 the Berlin regional court gave the two border soldiers a suspended sentence of 15 months. It never became clear who had fired the deadly shots. For this reason the sentence was for joint manslaughter. Michael Bittner also played a part in the "Politbüro" trial. The Berlin regional court accused Egon Krenz, Günter Schabowski and Günther Kleiber of his death as well as those of other victims of the Wall. On 25 August 1997 the court sentenced the three "Politbüro" members to between three and six and a half years in prison. Two years later the 5th (Leipzig) division of the Federal Supreme Court, as the court of appeal, confirmed the sentence. Egon Krenz in particular felt he had been treated unjustly. And Michael Bittner's mother? She often visits Edelhofdamm. "This is the only place where I can go sometimes and just gather my thoughts a bit, or perhaps be close to my son. Because, well, this is where he was shot. And I just don't know where he ended up."

TOUR 9

FROM FALKENSEER CHAUSSEE TO HEERSTRASSE

Falkenseer Chaussee – Finkenkruger Weg – Nennhauser Damm –
Hauptstrasse – Bergstrasse – Heerstrasse

Distance: 5 kilometres
Time: 1.5 hours

If there were ever a place on earth where the points of
the compass have been reversed, then it is here. Our tour
is therefore rather strange: the terrain on the west of our
route used to belong to the political "East", and that on
the "left" that is to the "east", strictly speaking was part of
the Spandau district of West Berlin.

When we get off the 137 bus at the Freudstrasse stop,
and go along Falkenseer Chaussee towards the signs
reading "Berlin Bezirk Spandau" and "Stadt Falkensee
Landkreis Havelland", we are approaching the westerly
city boundary of Berlin, where, up to 14 November 1989,
a concrete wall went across the road between Spandau
and the Albrechtshof estate in the GDR. The border area
left behind a strip of wasteland that is now gradually dis-
appearing between privately owned houses.

There is a stone block "in memory of the pre-1989
division" at the city boundary. Next to it, a tarmac road
winds its way past the Spandau allotments association
"Neu-Sternfeld" on the left and colonies of 'pioneer
plants' on the right. We will encounter these plants again
and again: birches and the brilliant yellow goldenrod,
which grew freely, protected by the Wall. British military
police and West Berlin police officers used to inspect the
border area on this tarmac road. But walkers and cyclists
were allowed to use the path too.

We reach Finkenkruger Weg, which has become a
cul-de-sac since the building of the Wall – with a nicely
paved turning-area. Here the erratic city boundary made

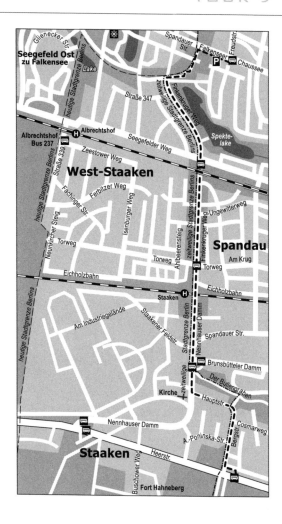

its way towards the south. From the road surface it is easy to see exactly where Berlin finished and the GDR began. The Berlin roadbuilders were only allowed to roll out their tar as far as the middle of the street, although the Wall itself stood several metres further back, behind the linden trees that line the street. However, the city boundary did not always go along here – and now it no longer does either. A strange story.

Future house-owners, living in West-Staaken, approach Finkenkruger Weg almost hesitantly. The sites were bought wholesale by property companies divided into

At the Potsdam Conference in 1945, the Western Allies made sure when they were dividing Berlin into sectors that each one included an airport. Johannisthal, later Schönefeld (Soviet Union), Tegel (France), Tempelhof (USA) and Gatow (Great Britain). However, Berlin's city boundary ran right across the Gatow landing-strip, so that it was partly in the Soviet-occupied zone. On 30 August 1945, the British and Soviet representatives, therefore, agreed to round off the city boundary so that the whole airport belonged to the British sector. In exchange control of the western part of Staaken – with the Staaken-Dallgow airport – was handed over to the Soviet military administration. Its civilian administration remained formally the responsibility of the Spandau town council, but was increasingly carried out by the East Berlin area authority, Mitte. In March 1950 a legal report confirmed that West-Staaken was no longer part of the British sector. On the morning of 2 February 1951 the GDR police moved into West-Staaken and subordinated it to the authority of the Mitte district (later to the council of the Nauen district). Thousands of residents of West-Staaken cleared out their houses and moved to West Berlin. In return, the GDR's Council of Ministers provided a million marks for rebuilding the infrastructure. New residents moved into the abandoned houses. In April 1951 barriers were erected in the centre of Staaken, and from May 1952 it was no longer possible to cross the border. West and East Staaken were finally divided. From 3 October 1990, West-Staaken once again belonged to the Spandau district. And once again many people lost their homes – the houses were returned to the former owners, who had moved away in 1951, or their heirs.

WEST-STAAKEN

small plots, which were then sold for houses to be built on them. In the course of building, they still come across foundations and concrete remains from the time of the Wall. Memories.

Finkenkruger Weg, corner of Street 347. A wooden cross, conifers, withered wreaths, the inscription: "Willi Block † 7. 2. 66". Here a 31-year-old man tried to squeeze through the barbed wire to Spandau. He managed to climb through one barrier, but got entangled in the second. For several minutes he hung there, trapped. Border soldiers observed him, approached – 30 in number – and far from helping him, they fired. Four bullets hit him, with fatal results. "The man was executed," said the presiding judge at the Berlin regional court on 1 February 1995, sentencing the commandant of the border regiment to three years in prison for attempted manslaughter. The public prosecutor's office lodged an appeal with the Federal Court, whose 5th "Strafsenat" made a fundamental judgement which was then the base for future cases in May 1996: border officers who ordered their troops to shoot were always to blame for the death of escapees, because through their orders they condoned the killing of such people.

Finkenkruger Weg, 11 September 1966. A Staaken family must have been quite surprised by some unexpected guests who came running into their garden while they were having coffee. Although under fire from border soldiers, two families had just used a bulldozer to shove the barbed wire and fence posts from the West Staaken side to the Spandau side of Finkenkruger Weg, and then happily jumped out of their armoured vehicle – right into the garden. The bulldozer was taken back to the GDR. But first, police counted the bullet holes: 48 altogether, none of them fatal.

The regional trains and inter-city expresses thunder towards Hamburg over the railway bridge behind Seegefelder Weg. This line was officially opened on 28 May 1995. Before then, no trains had passed through here for almost 34 years. The severing of the railway line had been well prepared. On 15 February 1954, when Falkensee

TOUR 9

station was connected to the newly created Berlin transport ring system East Berliners were able to reach the
Spandau district without going through West Berlin.
Nevertheless, from 1953 to 1958, during the rush hour
through trains would run from Falkensee via Albrechtshof and Spandau to Friedrichstrasse in East Berlin –
without stopping. Passengers were not permitted to leave
the train in the west sectors. The end of the S-Bahn traffic came with the order by the GDR's minister for transport "that from 1 p. m. on 13. 8.1961 the departure of all
S-Bahn trains to West Berlin is to be cancelled. From
1.30 p. m. no S-Bahn trains from Spandau-West can be
permitted to enter. Long-distance trains to and from
West Berlin via Falkensee will run according to the timetable as before and will not be subject to any restrictions."
For almost two months there was still a shuttle service
between Falkensee and Albrechtshof station. After that,
the Albrechtshof stop fell into disuse. Since August 1990
regional trains have been running again; as before, the
S-Bahn does not run through here.

Long-distance trains were cancelled on 5 December
1961, five days earlier than planned. The reason for the
urgency was a curious one. Harry Deterling, engine driver
for the Deutsche Reichsbahn, had applied to the party
secretary of his company for special shiftwork. They were
happy to assign Harry and his fireman, Hartmut Lichy, the
local train from Oranienburg via Nauen to Albrechtshof.
The train departed punctually at 19.33, but did not arrive
according to the timetable. The last stop was Falkensee.
In Albrechtshof the train steamed past the amazed station
staff. Border barriers were disregarded. There was an
emergency signal to the level-crossing attendant, telling
him to turn his handle immediately. The guard tugged at
the emergency brake – with limited success – for Deterling had let off the steam. At 21.03 the train reached the
area of Spandau. It stopped between stations. 25 happy
escapees, friends and relatives of the two men in the driver's cab jumped out of the train. The passengers also included a GDR police officer. Conscious of his duty, he
warned them that leaving the train between stations was

forbidden. Only then did he realise where he was. Grumbling, he returned to Albrechtshof, together with the guard and five passengers who had also travelled further than they wished.

On the very next night, the rails of the "Hamburger Bahn" were cut. After this there was only one rail link to the Federal Republic, the one via Griebnitzsee (see Tour 10, From Glienicker Brücke to Griebnitzsee S-Bahn station (Steinstücken) in the south-west of Berlin. Not until 27 September 1976 did the first train run again via Spandau without being diverted to Hamburg, but then it no longer went via Albrechtshof, but a few hundred metres to the south, via Staaken. We will soon come to the site of the border railway station there.

The old border area can still be seen at the western edge of Finkenkruger Weg. The eastern, Spandau side is adorned by the garden town of Staaken, an estate of 804 homes in 298 detached houses and 146 houses converted into flats built between 1914 and 1917 to a design by Paul Schmitthenner. Torweg is its main street. This is where the residents of the garden town celebrated "their" border opening on 23 March 1990.

Trains are running again under Nennhauser Damm-Brücke. The tracks of the high-speed trains to Braunschweig are on the right, where the Lehrter Bahn used to run, and next to it is the Staaken stop for local trains. There was an S-Bahn station in Staaken to the left of the bridge – after the building of the Wall this was the terminus. In September 1980 it was closed down. From 1976 the transit trains to and from Hamburg stopped at the border station on the right of the bridge to allow the GDR customs officers to get on and off. For several hundred metres the tracks led to the west between walls, so no one could jump on. On 27 September 1998 Berlin was linked up to the high-speed network of the Deutsche Bahn. The first plans for this had been laid before 1989, but had failed as a result of the doubts of the GDR authorities. Those plans mean that today the long-distance trains to the West go as quickly as possible by the shortest route.

Just behind the railway line, immediately next to the former border areas, is today's Linden primary school.
Pupils and teachers were only allowed to enter the
school with special permission. The main part of the primary school is a complex of buildings from the 1930s,
which are under a preservation order. The arrival of many
young families in the last few years made additional
buildings necessary, including the large sports hall. Opposite this, on the corner of Nennhauser Damm and
Spandauer Strasse, there is a restaurant with the appropriate name "Grenz-Eck" (Border Corner) which also
has seats outside. From its narrow terrace the "border
corner" can no longer be seen; what can be observed is
the gradual construction in Staakener Feldstrasse of
house after house in the Spandauer Mühlenviertel by
the "Gemeinnützige Wohnungsbau AG" (architects:
Garsztecki und Hartmann). On 1 July 1988, after a territory purchase deal between the Berlin Senate and the

Staaken: "Border
corridor" for the
transit trains to
and from Ham-
burg (1985)

GDR government, Nennhauser Damm, Finkenkruger Weg and Bergstrasse (which we will come to later) were entirely absorbed into the Spandau district. Then all the streets were accessible. However Brunsbütteler Damm still ended right next to the Wall. The large turning-place was where the buses of the "Berliner Verkehrsgesellschaft" (BVG) terminated.

The bright white village church, built in the 14th century, is the centre-point of Staaken. To the north, the churchyard ended at the border area that was not far from the church, directly to Nennhauser Damm. Only residents were permitted to enter, only from the direction of the GDR and only with special authorisation. After two years of restoration, the church has been used again since September 2002.

The creation of the border meant that the parish was also divided. The parish of Alt-Staaken/Albrechtshof belonged to the district of Falkensee, while the West Berliners stayed in the Spandau district. In 2000, the Berlin-Brandenburg church restored the old parish. The parish priest Norbert Rauer was sceptical: "As though nothing had happened here between 1951 and 1990."

There are plenty of places of remembrance to be found in the little church, even more in its churchyard and the old village square. There is the obligatory war memorial to the sons lost in the First World War by "the grateful people of Staaken". The residents of West Staaken were not given much time to commemorate their dead of 1939 to 1945 with a memorial stone; for after 1951 this was forbidden by their new rulers. On the other hand, there is a memorial to the fallen soldiers of the Red Army, which liberated Staaken from the Fascists on 25 April 1945. The story of its creation is a strange one. History was literally turned upside-down. A memorial stone of 1901, which the worthy farmers had had carved for the 200th anniversary of the elevation of Prussia to the status of a kingdom, was simply adapted and given a new identity, in German and Russian (see the information plaque).

A black cross and a mulberry tree, planted in the churchyard on 17 June 1993, are reminders of the division of Staaken in 1951 and reunification in 1990. A plaque in the churchyard wall refers to the celebrations in Staaken on the occasion of the jubilee in 1913 of Emperor Wilhelm II: "Hail to our ruler!" Five years later he had lost his realm; he had abdicated.

Our tour now takes us to the left into Hauptstrasse. We imagine that we can smell country air between the old, low-built houses and under the mighty trees with their branches entwined. But a wooden cross at the end of Hauptstrasse, at the corner of Bergstrasse, immediately brings us back into the modern age. On 9 December 1961 a 20-year-old student died here. Dieter Wohlfahrt, who was trying to help the mother of a young woman to escape, was about to cut through the barbed wire when the border guards discovered him and shot him. The young Austrian bled to death for over two hours — no help was forthcoming from either east or west. Sebastian Haffner, a famous German writer, commented: "Berliners on both sides are unwilling to accept as a fact the monstrous nature of the Wall, either *de jure* or *de facto*. The Allies, however, and, under pressure from them, the West Berlin authorities, behave in practice more and more as though the Wall were already recognised both *de facto* and *de jure*. Where are the times when the photograph of a task force marksman who had shot an escapee dead in the Teltow canal was plastered all over Berlin, and 10,000 marks offered for his arrest? Today the border police fish the body of one of their victims out of the ice-cold December water every few days, and no one takes any notice any more."

It is only a few more metres along Bergstrasse to Heerstrasse. In the past, one of the four border checkpoints between West Berlin and the GDR extended across the wide stretch of wasteland, on which now and again a circus tent is put up. From here the main road no. 5 went to Lauenburg and Hamburg. Even cyclists were able to use this road, if they were in training and fit enough: from 1958 the 237 kilometres had to be completed in one day. On 22 December 1987 a new border checkpoint for transit traffic came into operation on the new Berlin-Hamburg motorway. Staaken remained open for travel into the GDR. The West Berlin police had its administrative office for border clearance in a brightly painted house at number 529–531 Heerstrasse. Today it accommodates the studios and workshops of the 'Arbeitskreis Spandauer Künstler" (Study Group for Artists of Spandau).

The hill above the checkpoint was once dominated by Fort Hahneberg, built from 1882 to 1888, the last artillery fort to be built in Germany – part of a defence line drawn around the fortress of Spandau. After all, this was where the hoard of gold that the French had to pay after the war of 1870/71 was stored. But that is yet another story. It is time for us to wait for the number 149 bus, which will take us back into the city centre.

TOUR 10

FROM GLIENICKER BRÜCKE TO GRIEBNITZSEE S-BAHN STATION (STEINSTÜCKEN)

Glienicker Brücke – Königstrasse – Wilhelm-Leuschner-Strasse – Waldmüllerstrasse – Lankestrasse – Wasserstrasse – BUGA-Weg 2002 (former border area) – Griebnitzsee S-Bahn station (Karl-Marx-Strasse – August-Bebel-Strasse – Steinstrasse – Am Landeplatz – Teltower Strasse – Studentendorf – Griebnitzsee S-Bahn station)

Distance: 5.5 kilometres (7.5 kilometres)
Time: 2 hours (2.5 hours)

For Alexander von Humboldt the view from Glienicker Brücke was one of the most beautiful in the world. As he had travelled around almost the whole world, we should believe him. But in 1980 his opinion would very likely have been quite different. This probably would not have been because of the shape of the bridge, which was 146 metres long, built between 1904 and 1907 over the Havel, and bombed ten days before the end of the Second World War. Rather he would have wondered why the Brandenburg government christened it the "Bridge of Unity" on its reopening in December 1949, when it was already closed to traffic from the Potsdam side on 26 May 1952. And Humboldt would most certainly have objected to the high concrete wall on the banks of the Havel, which denied citizens the freedom of movement that he, as a subject of the Prussian kings, had enjoyed to such a high degree – not to speak of the destruction of the landscape (since 1990 on the UNESCO World Cultural Heritage List). But all this is speculation. Let us keep to the facts. We will begin our search at the Glienicker Brücke bus and tram stop.

From 1952 up to 10 November 1989, when the normal traffic was once more rolling over Glienicker Brücke, only Allied military staff and a small group of individuals with special permission (as well as diplomats after 1985) had been allowed to use it. It was a place of peace. Most of the time. Due to its remote location this steel bridge was an important 'hinge' in the Iron Curtain, which was lifted here from time to time; sometimes to bring the coffins of Soviet World War soldiers to Potsdam, sometimes to bring the body of a US spy who had been shot dead back to the American sector, or to return aircrafts used by escapees.

Worldwide attention was attracted by Francis Gary Powers and Rudolf Ivanovich Abel. One of them had triggered off the U2 affair in 1960 when he was shot down over Sverdlovsk in his spy plane, while the other had held the strings of the Soviet spy network until his cover was blown in 1957. In the grey dawn of 10 February 1962,

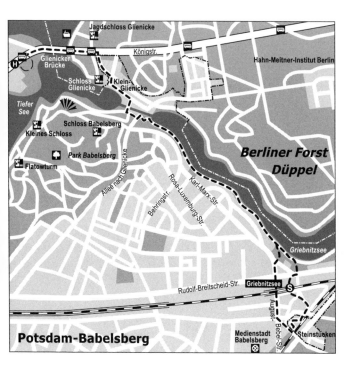

TOUR 10

Powers and Abel, released to freedom on Glienicker Brücke, exchanged limousines. At midday on 12 June 1985 the same spot was at its busiest once again. There was a further exchange of agents: four GDR spies for 23 US spies from prisons in the GDR and Poland. And finally, on the morning of 11 February 1986, Anatoly Sharansky, sentenced to 13 years in prison for treason as a Soviet civil rights campaigner, was freed in exchange for five spies from the East and one helper.

And then, on 10 March 1988, there was a top class-escape. Three men from Babelsberg stole a lorry and filled it with empty gas cylinders to weigh it down. At 2 am this monstrous vehicle approached Glienicker Brücke through the dark Berliner Strasse, accelerated, drove faster and faster, two Soviet guards called "stoj, stoj" (stop, stop), then were forced to jump to one side, and the vehicle burst through iron barriers and everything else that was in its way. Only when it was well into West Berlin did the colossus come to a halt and out got the three men from Babelsberg.

What is left of the myth of the Cold War? Graffiti in Cyrillic script on the southern colonnades. Marks made by the barriers in the road surface. The bronze sculpture "Nike '89" by Wieland Förster, unveiled in 1999, ten years after the opening of the bridge. There is a faded white stripe right across the middle of the bridge: West on one side, East on the other (the different road surfaces show more clearly than the road markings where the states of Brandenburg and Berlin meet today). There is a turning-place on the Berlin side of the bridge: there was a cul-de-sac, a terminus here.

Let us once again enjoy the unobstructed view of the landscape at the Havel, in the middle of which buoys were once anchored to mark the border. On the far shore of Jungfernsee we are struck by the "Italian" Church of Our Saviour at Sakrow (built between 1841 and 1844 by Ludwig Persius), which used to be inaccessible in the border area and was succumbing to dry rot. In 1984/85, on the initiative of the "Tagesspiegel" news-paper (which donated half the cost), the church was restored, and Mass was celebrated here again for the first time on Christmas Eve 1989, attracting an enormous congregation. The English-Norman Schloss Babelsberg (built from 1834 to 1849 to the plans of Karl Friedrich Schinkel, Ludwig Persius and Johann Heinrich Strack) towers across the shore of Glienicker Lake. The view of the park (designed by Peter Joseph Lenné and Hermann Fürst von Pückler-Muskau) was ruined by the high Wall directly on the bank. Hidden behind that concrete mass, the visitor to the park was no longer "lord of the view", an axiom of Lenné's gardening principles.

Königstrasse leads us further through Prussia's Arcadia. On the left – again in "Italian" style – is Schloss Klein-Glienicke (built from 1825 to 1828 by Karl Friedrich Schinkel). We can see a rotunda in the castle park right next to Glienicker Brücke. The name of the rotunda "Große Neugierde" (great curiosity) explains its function. The park of the hunting lodge extends to the right of Bundesstrasse. At the end of it we turn right into Möwenstrasse and walk along the park wall, which, together with a "modern" wall running in front of it, formed the border between East and West. We are now in the village of Klein-Glienicke.

The courtyard of the Glienicke hunting lodge could not be entered from its promenade, Waldmüllerstrasse. The ornamented door was barred with barbed wire. The hunting horn had not sounded here for a long time. The mansion that the Elector of Brandenburg, Friedrich Wilhelm, had had built between 1677 and 1682, was given its present exterior at the end of the 19th century, this time in "French" Baroque. Its bare interior was designed by Max Taut in 1963. Today the house is an international youth community centre.

The spirit of pedagogic reform had already 'wafted' through the building in the 19th century. Wilhelm Carl Christian von Türk (born on 8 January 1774) had bought the Glienicke hunting lodge in 1827 and founded a "Civilian Orphanage for Boys" there as a counterpart to the military orphanage in Potsdam. Since 1807 he had

KLEIN-
GLIENICKE

In 1920, when Greater Berlin was made up of a number of towns and communities, Klein-Glienicke was not among them. It was an old village to which Prince Carl of Prussia gave shape, above all through the ten Swiss-style servants' houses, built between 1863 and 1867 (four of them still exist). When the Teltow canal was built in the years 1900 to 1906, a cutting was created from Griebnitzsee to Glienicker Lake. This separated Klein-Glienicke from Babelsberg, although they were connected by a bridge. Böttcherberg, Klein-Glienicke's local 'mountain', was bought by Prince Carl in 1824. Like the hunting lodge and Glienicke Park, in 1920 it was also under the administration of Berlin. Two sites in the village also belonged to Berlin and a section of Königstrasse to Klein-Glienicke, which had been part of Potsdam since 1939. The situation could hardly be more confusing.

When the Allies were drawing up definitions of their territories in 1945, they based them on the city limits of Berlin as they were in 1920. The complex situation at Böttcherberg with its odd corners and enclaves became a problem when the border was sealed off in 1952, and after 1961 when the village was surrounded by a wall. From Babelsberg there was only one access route, the bridge, which was guarded. Access was granted only by special permission. The inhabitants of Klein-Glienicke were treated with suspicion – there was a danger of their escaping. Some were relocated. Those who stayed behind were mainly elderly people, as one sees from the old people's home in Wilhelm-Leuschner-Strasse, now standing empty. One plan was to incorporate the village into West Berlin by exchanging territories. Instead, in 1971 Berlin gave up its two sites in the village, some 3,000 square metres. Access restrictions to Klein-Glinicke were not lifted until the end of 1989.

been a teacher at Pestalozzi's educational establishment in Herten, and in 1815 he became "Royal Prussian Schools Councillor" in Frankfurt on the Oder, in 1817 in Potsdam. When he died on 30 July 1846, he had become known as the "Pestalozzi of Brandenburg". He was buried in Klein-Glienicke. His grave is the oldest in the cemetery of the protestant church community in Babelsberg.

The intersection of Wilhelm-Leuschner-Strasse is not far from the gates of the mansion. If we look along it at the end of the street on both sides, we can make out the path cut across it by the Wall, now totally overgrown. Where the Wall cut through the cemetery, some of the graves of children had to be transferred. The neo-Gothic Klein-Glienicke chapel (built in 1881 by Reinhold Persius) was saved from dilapidation. It was restored from 1990 to 1999 with the help of private donations. Its distinctive features are the interior decoration and the Schuke organ. Uecumenical services are held here regularly under the symbolic motto "Overcoming borders".

In Waldmüllerstrasse we face a difficult decision. Should we go straight on, then keep to the left and explore the second, somewhat "mountainous" corner of the enclave which, 'displaced' by the Wall, intruded into Berlin? The streets called Am Böttcherberg, Am Waldrand and Wannseestrasse define the course of the border (Am Waldrand was where the border to Berlin was opened on 17 March 1990). Or should we head for number 4 Waldmüllerstrasse, and call in for a drink?

Here is "Bürgershof". Opened in 1875 and enlarged year by year, this hotel and restaurant, with its own boathouse, large banqueting hall, terrace and steamboat landing-stage became the largest tourist attraction far and wide. In 1961 it was in the border area, ten years later the site was expropriated and the main building was demolished for border security reasons. In the beer garden (the tables are not laid, and we are allowed to bring our own food) we sit under a high five-pronged spotlight, which used to light up the border. The present tenant has been running the restaurant since 1992. So far he has invested only the bare minimum, for the title to the property is still not clear – will it have to be returned or not?

At the traffic lights at the end of Waldmüllerstrasse we turn right into Lankestrasse and cross the narrow

TOUR 10

Parkbrücke over to Neu-Babelsberg. Permits are no longer required, and the inspector's hut that stood on the right at the other end of the bridge is no longer there. A winding road leads through the avenue via Glienicke to Wasserstrasse. At the end of this street, we follow the sign "BUGA-Weg 2001" and make the deep descent into the former border area. The border soldiers used to carry out their patrols on the asphalted road where we are now walking.

Buoys mark the border in the middle of the lake (1985)

The northern half of Griebnitzsee belongs to Berlin. The border passes through the middle of the lake. West Berlin's water-sports enthusiasts came from Wannsee to practise their sports at Griebnitzsee. "Particular care was always required. Woe betide a rowing crew if they passed over the buoys anchored in the middle to mark the border! The crews of the GDR's border boats often reacted aggressively," says Gerhard Wünsch of the Berlin rowing club Astoria.

The lake was inaccessible to the general public and the residents from the south. At its banks the border area was levelled off. The vegetation we are passing has only been growing here since reunification. Some eccentric property owners use parts of the old metal fence as a border for their own property. Others regard the former hinterland wall, the original metal fence with concrete posts, moved back somewhat, as their own property border. The tarmac road turns into a sandy path. Occasionally above us we catch a glimpse of one of the villas once occupied by entrepreneurs, bankers and film stars. They did not have far to go to work. In the 1930s Babelsberg was "UfA City", the German Hollywood.

Immediately after the war – UfA's days of glory were over for the time being – the negotiators of the Potsdam Conference (15 July to 2 August 1945) moved into the beautiful villas by the lake. Stalin lived in Kaiserstrasse (today number 27 Karl-Marx-Strasse), Churchill and, after him, Attlee in Ringstrasse (today 23 Virchowstrasse). Truman was at number 2 Kaiserstrasse. After about two kilometres, by following the right-hand fork in the road up the hill, we reach his "Little White House" with the two widely curved gable roofs, mansard bay windows, terrace and extensive garden. The house was built from 1891 to 1892 for the Berlin publisher Carl Müller-Grote. A plaque at the door of number 2 Karl-Marx-Strasse, commemorates the US president. Today the villa is used by the Friedrich-Naumann-Stiftung, which has links with the FDP (Freie Demokratische Partei).

Wandering further alongside the lake, after 500 metres we go down a flight of steps and reach Griebnitzsee S-Bahn station. Walking past Truman House, we come to a major crossroads. Leaving the timber-built post office building on the right, we cross Rudolf-Breitscheid-Strasse to August-Bebel-Strasse. About 200 metres after the railway subway, Steinstrasse branches off sharply to the left. In Rote-Kreuz-Strasse we are on former border territory once again. The Wall ran along Rote-Kreuz-Strasse and turned off into Steinstrasse, which ended in a cul-de-sac. Bits of mortar on the left-hand pavement of Steinstrasse show exactly where the Wall used to be.

A little footpath behind number 28 Steinstrasse takes us to what was once Berlin's best known exclave (a part of a state enclosed in foreign territory), Steinstücken.

The footpath leads to the spot where there was a helicopter landing place from 1963 to 1976. This is recorded by a memorial with two vertically placed rotor blades, and a climbing frame shaped like a helicopter on the playground. The US Air Force's helicopters regularly dropped off military policemen there, brought the Governing Mayor of Berlin; and at Christmas, to the delight of the children, Santa Claus even arrived by helicopter. However, there was never any need for the helicopter pilots

STEIN-
STÜCKEN

In 1887 the farmer Bernhard Beyer bought 12 hectares of land, known as Steinstücken. Beyer lived in Kohlhasenbrück, later part of Wannsee, which was annexed to Greater Berlin in 1920. Thus Steinstücken also belonged to Berlin – 1,200 metres from the city limits. This did not become a problem until after 1945. Which currency was to be used? What food vouchers were valid? On 18 October 1951, the GDR police tried to clarify the situation. They occupied Steinstücken. After protests by the USA they withdrew again, but after June 1952 only residents of Steinstücken were allowed in the exclave. On 21 August 1961 barbed wire was put up all round it (and from 1963/64 a wall). A three-metre-wide, closely observed path remained as the only connection to West Berlin. It was to be used only by the 150 residents of Steinstücken. Three US military policemen, who took over from each other by helicopter, were regularly on "outpost" duty in the exclave. In 1971, representatives of the Berlin senate and the GDR government negotiated about Steinstücken. Behind soundproof doors they discussed a plan to exchange Steinstücken temporarily for Klein-Glienicke and relocate the residents. The eventual solution was more humane. By exchanging territories on 20 December 1971, West Berlin received a 20-metre-wide area where an unsupervised road could be built between Kohlhasenbrück and Steinstücken. This road (the continuation Bernhard-Beyer-Strasse) was completed on 29 August 1972, thus ending the area's exclave status.

Playground on a
former helicopter
landing place
(2002)

to organise an airlift. Even though certain things were unavailable in the isolated exclave, and there were various causes for complaint, for example over the pesticides sprayed by aircraft over the border area – and thus over the gardens – it never came to a blockade. One last helicopter, by the way, landed on 29 September 1990, four days before the completion of German unification. It aroused memories, for instance of the American "boys" who had married women from Steinstücken.

From the helicopter landing place we now travel to the left as far as Teltower Strasse, and follow this to the right as far as Stahnsdorfer Strasse. The houses on both sides of Teltower Strasse belong to Steinstücken, those on the opposite side of Stahnsdorfer Strasse to Potsdam. After reunification a students' village was created here. Passing through this (Stahnsdorfer Strasse on the right and left at the entrance to the car park) we come to Griebnitzsee S-Bahn station with its many rails.

This place, where our tour ends, has historical significance. From 1961 to 1976 Griebnitzsee station was Berlin's only border checkpoint for all interzone and through rail traffic (see the information board in the entrance hall). All the trains from Berlin stopped here, were checked and then continued, if possible without further stops, as far as the stations at the border of the Federal Republic: depending on the direction, these were (until 1976) Schwanheide, Marienborn, Gerstungen and Probstzella. After the train was checked again, it was allowed to enter the Federal Republic. When the transit agreement of 1972 came into force, the procedure was simplified. The trains stopped at the border stations only to allow the GDR customs officers to get in and out (transit visas were issued during the journey) and to give tracker dogs time to sniff for escapees clinging on under the carriages. The significance of this little S-Bahn station with its centuries-old roof supports on the platform is no longer obvious, but people still wonder why there is so much unnecessary space between the rails.

Berlin: open city
The City on Exhibition
The Tours

Edited by the Berliner Festspiele and
the Architektenkammer Berlin
288 pages, with descriptions of 600 buildings,
over 250 photographs,
51 plans, 11 folding maps and
an index of architects and places.
ISBN 3-87584-773-3

€ 14,90

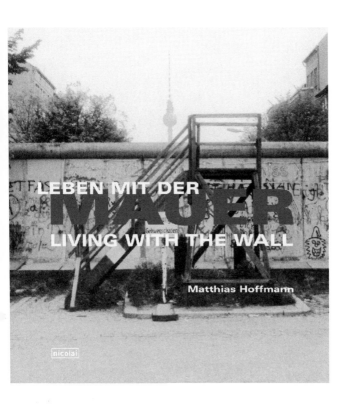

Matthias Hoffmann
Living with the Wall/
Leben mit der Mauer
(German/English)

132 pages,
87 black- and-white photographs
bound
ISBN 3-87584-607-9

€ 19,90